MOTOR SAILING

Other titles of interest

Sails (6th edition): *Jeremy Howard-Williams*
ISBN 0-229-11824-0
An encylopedic volume covering every type of sail.

Rigging: *Enrico Sala*
ISBN 0-229-11817-8
Illustrated with 150 colour diagrams, this book will assist all DIY enthusiasts
to maintain and improve all aspects of rigging on their craft.

Boat Electrical Systems: *Dag Pike*
ISBN 0-7136-3451-0
This very practical, straightforward guide demystifies the subject for all owners
wishing to fit out a boat, install new electronic equipment or simply sort out an
annoying electrical problem.

Boatowner's Mechanical and Electrical Manual: *Nigel Calder*
ISBN 0-7136-3251-8
This complete DIY manual takes novice and experienced boat owners through
minor to major repairs of all mechanical and electrical gear.

Propeller Handbook: *Dave Gerr*
ISBN 0-7136-5751-0
A practical aid for the mechanic, engineer, boat-builder, naval architect
or yachtsman for all boats.

Fitting Out (4th edition): *J D Sleightholme*
ISBN 0-7136-3558-4
Covers every aspect of preparing a boat for sea, from the bare essentials needed
to make a safe delivery passage, to a total fit-out.

Laying Up Your Boat: *H Janssen*
ISBN 0-7136-3456-1
The pros and cons, risks and costs are analysed carefully, and advice is given on
a whole range of matters in a straightforward manner to help anxious owners
lay up their boats safely and without problems.

Osmosis and the Care and Repair of Glassfibre Yachts: *Tony Staton-Bevan*
ISBN 0-7136-3513-4
The prevention and cure of osmosis are dealt with and owners advised as to
how to detect potential trouble spots and repair the damage.

Effective Skippering: *John Myatt*
ISBN 0-7136-3460-X
A complete manual for yacht owners covering every aspect of yacht
management.

Heavy Weather Sailing (4th edition): *K Adlard Coles*
Revised by Peter Bruce
ISBN 0-7136-3431-6
The established authority on the subject of handling sailing and motor vessels
in gale and storm conditions.

MOTOR SAILING

Cruising under sail and power

DAG PIKE

ADLARD COLES NAUTICAL
LONDON

This edition published 1993 by Adlard Coles Nautical
an imprint of A & C Black (Publishers) Ltd
35 Bedford Row, London WC1R 4JH

Copyright © Dag Pike 1976, 1993

First edition published by Stanford Maritime Ltd 1976
Second edition published by Adlard Coles Nautical 1993

ISBN 0-7136-3695-5

Typeset in Palatino by Falcon Graphic Art Ltd
Printed and bound in Great Britain by
Butler and Tanner Ltd., Frome Somerset

A CIP catalogue record for this book is available from the
British Library.

Acknowledgements

My sincere thanks are due to the many motor sailer builders
who helped with information and photographs for this book. In
particular I should mention Northshore Yachts and
Volvo Penta.

My thanks also to Jess Bennett for some of the drawings and to
Gina Haines, my secretary, who typed the manuscript, the
index, and helped in a thousand other ways.

CONTENTS

CHAPTER 1

▬

THE WORLD OF MOTOR SAILING

Welcome to the world of motor sailing. This is a world which belongs to the cruising yachtsman; a world where sail and power are combined to offer improved safety and convenience, where high performance gives way to comfortable cruising, and where seamanship and common sense are the guiding factors.

What is a motor sailer?

Although a motor sailer is easily distinguished from a motor boat by its mast and sails, there is no such clear-cut division between many sailing cruisers and a motor sailer. The latter will tend to have an enclosed wheelhouse, or at least a steering shelter, but the real difference, in my opinion, lies in performance.

A motor sailer must have the ability to proceed under sail or motor in rough conditions. In this it differs from the auxiliary sailing yacht, where the motor is mainly used for manoeuvring in harbour or in calm conditions: the low powered engine with its single propeller tends to run out of steam quite quickly in rough conditions, and it cannot always make progress to windward in a fresh breeze. At the other end of the spectrum is the motor cruiser with steadying sails (certainly a rare type of craft these days), but in this case the sails are for steadying the boat and are not intended for propulsion, so again this does not properly fit the definition of a motor sailer. A good definition might be that a motor sailer is a yacht which, by using either sails or engine independently, is able to make progress to windward in adverse conditions.

Most sailing yachts are obviously able to make progress to windward under sail alone, as long as they have a reasonably efficient set of sails and a hull shape which doesn't make too much leeway. But it is when we look at the second aspect of my definition – making progress to windward under motor in adverse conditions – that many sailing yachts would fail to qualify. Head winds and seas can quickly make a small and inadequate engine unsuitable, so in order to meet my definition of a motor sailer, the craft should have a powerful engine and a propulsion system to match.

The history of the motor sailer

Historically the motor sailer is not new. When engines were first put into boats in the last century, the sails were generally retained because those early engines were not particularly reliable and the sails offered an alternative means of propulsion in the event of engine failure; they could also be used to improve the economy of operation when the weather was fair. This combination of power and sail in one vessel was used on big ships as well as small, and the naval expression, 'Up funnel, down sail', is a legacy from the period of transition from sail to power, which spanned about fifty years.

The auxiliary engine fitted to early yachts was of very low power and provided performance which was only really adequate for harbour manoeuvring. Nowadays, though, sailing yachts are fitted with larger engines, and perhaps more importantly with an effective propulsion system; it is this combination which categorises the motor sailer.

The true motor sailer, however, was developed more from the fishing

A traditional wooden motor sailer showing its fishing boat origins. Note the large wheelhouse with reverse sloping forward windows and a raised forecastle deck. *Photo: Millers*

boat concept, where sails were retained for many years after engines were installed: today we still find steadying sails fitted to fishing boats, even though they are modern in design in every other respect. The earliest motor sailers were developed from the motor fishing vessel, and were thus very much motor orientated: the famous Fifers, which are recognised by many as the predecessors of the modern motor sailer, can trace a direct ancestry to fishing boats; indeed they were developed and built by the same yards that built their fishing cousins. The similarities between the hull shapes of the two types is very pronounced, particularly above the waterline, whilst below the waterline the motor sailer tended to develop both a reduced draft in order to improve its cruising capabilities, and finer lines to enhance its sailing capabilities. It is from these two diverse starting points – early leisure craft and working vessels – that the modern motor sailer has developed.

Characteristics

A distinctive type of motor sailer, which was developed largely from the fishing boats or similar seaworthy designs, was the 50/50. This was a forerunner of the modern motor sailer, its name indicating that it was half motor and half sail, although it in fact had a strong emphasis on power. In the early days of development of this class of motor sailer, potential owners were faced with the choice of having the emphasis on power or on sail: today, with modern developments and the use of modern materials, an effective combination of both is possible.

In the USA, the 'deck house sail boat' certainly comes into the category of motor sailer in terms of appearance. This boat has the characteristic wheelhouse or steering shelter, offering more comfort and protection. Although its name does not suggest that it performs as well under motor as under sail, this tends to be an accepted feature of these yachts. An alternative name for this type of vessel is the 'pilot house sail boat', and it is interesting that both these names have a traditional ring about them, reflecting the traditional qualities of many motor sailer designs.

Another term used in sales literature for this category of boat is the 'fully powered sailing cruiser'. The aim of such a title is obviously to get away from the sometimes staid image which motor sailers engender, and it certainly describes very well some of the modern craft which come into the motor sailer category, although the name tends to refer to those motor sailers which are more sail than power orientated.

It may be surprising to find that a yacht which occupies a midway position between power and sailing craft has developed such a definite character of its own. For a middle-of-the-road type of yacht the motor sailer is surprisingly individual, and externally has many features which create this individuality. The wheelhouse or steering shelter is, as I have mentioned, one of the more obvious characteristics, although this is not necessarily an essential feature of the design. Perhaps less obvious, but in many cases more characteristic, is the sheer line of the deck. On many modern power boats and sailing yachts the line has moved from the traditional sheer, which rises at bow and stern and drops away amidships, to be replaced by either a straight line or even a reverse sheer. These changes in the sheer line reflect the requirement to create more space within the hull in order to provide comfortable accommodation, whilst on most motor sailers the addition of the wheelhouse or steering shelter provides additional accommodation without necessarily altering the sheer line. So we find that most modern motor sailers still retain the conventional sheer line, which produces a very attractive hull shape with a direct relationship to more traditional yacht designs.

Every boat show produces new sail and power boats which reflect greater and greater extremes of design. Whilst increasingly more boating tends to take place in sheltered waters, these extremes can be tolerated because they can still perform in these conditions. For the more adventurous cruising yachtsman, however, the more conservative approach of the motor sailer can have considerable appeal: I would suggest that one of the main attractions of the motor sailer is its seamanlike and traditional appearance – a protest, perhaps, against the continuing quest for speed and mass acceptability.

Some designers are now attempting to glamorise the motor sailer, perhaps at the expense of its seamanlike characteristics. Progress in design is important, but there is a growing body of serious yachtsmen who take safety and seaworthiness seriously, and do not want to be restricted in their cruising programme by the design of their yacht. They want a sound, seaworthy vessel in which they don't have to spend their time at sea listening nervously to every weather forecast.

With modern technology the compromises which have to be made with a motor sailer are becoming less restrictive. Modern, powerful diesel engines are available in a compact package which makes the engine easier to accommodate in a small space without intruding on the accommodation too much. Modern hull construction materials allow hulls to be built to lighter scantlings whilst still retaining adequate strength. Tremendous strides have been made in the development of masts, sails and rigging, particularly in the area of self-furling systems. These aspects all give the designer much more flexibility to optimise the design for a particular purpose, and for the single-handed or two-handed cruising yachtsman, the boat becomes much easier to handle, which in turn can improve the safety and seaworthiness of the vessel.

Modern technology has also brought about other design developments. One such was the planing motor sailer, which enjoyed a very brief period of popularity. Here was a class of boat in which, under power, speeds of up to 30 knots could be achieved, but which would still have adequate performance under sail. It was quite a design challenge to develop such a craft, but commercially it was not a success simply because there were few people who wanted to travel at 30 knots under power and who also wanted to sail.

This motor sailer has roller main and jib to give simple sail handling. The main rolls into the boom when not in use. *Photo: Scanyachts*

Another modern development which has stood the test of time much better and looks like taking over a large sector of the motor sailer market is the catamaran. This design offers considerable space for accommodation and is often fitted with twin engines. Many modern catamaran designs certainly come within the motor sailer category and are a good example of how modern design and materials can add a new dimension to an old concept.

As the motor sailer has developed in recent years, we are finding that what might be termed the 'motor orientated' motor sailer is tending to disappear in favour of designs where there is a stronger emphasis on sailing capability. This change reflects the ability to incorporate powerful engines into what are basically sailing yachts, and designers are finding that there is less need to compromise on the aspects of either sail or motor whilst still being able to obtain a good performance under sail and power. This does not, however, mean that the motor orientated motor sailer is dead by a long way; there is still a strong body of yachtsmen who find great aesthetic appeal in this type of craft, which more than justifies boat builders still producing this type of design.

Much of the present appeal of the motor sailer in its modern form comes from its restrained, dignified, yet eager shape, and its ability to perform well in different roles. Some of this appeal may be lost if the more glamorous aspects of design take over, but clever designers will be able to achieve the best of both worlds and recognise the value of the aesthetic appeal of the motor sailer concept. Because yachts are largely bought for pleasure, the aesthetic aspects of design are vitally important, and the traditional appeal of the motor sailer will keep a strong body of yachtsmen loyal to this design concept.

Advantages

Having established that the motor sailer is a unique category of yacht, what are its advantages, apart from the obvious one of being able to make progress efficiently either under sail or power? The main one has to be the fact that the motor sailer probably represents the ideal cruising boat for those who have to keep to a timetable and meet the conflicting requirements of business and pleasure. The motor sailer doesn't offer immunity from bad weather, but it certainly offers greater flexibility in being able to cope with it, so the motor sailer owner will probably find that he has to make fewer changes to his plans because of changing weather conditions. Motor sailer owners are not forced to run for shelter at the first sign of deteriorating conditions and so will be more relaxed about planning a weekend sailing even if they have to get back for work on Monday morning.

Motor sailers can also make a very suitable craft for open sea passages where the duration can be counted in days rather than hours. On this sort of passage, the yacht can be a considerable distance from the nearest shelter, but the owner can be reasonably confident that he has a boat

A low profile wheelhouse allows a low sail rig and gives sweet lines, but the liferaft on the foredeck obstructs visibility from the wheelhouse.

which will be able to cope with most conditions. Provided the boat is well constructed and the wheelhouse sound, then bad weather can be faced with reasonable equanimity – if some discomfort!

By having adequate power and a rig which can be relied on, the motor sailer owner is not wholly dependent on either. Without wind good progress can be made under motor, whilst the peace and quiet of sailing can be enjoyed when the wind is favourable. With the combination of sail and power, heaving to, if conditions demand it, is a much safer operation, and with a powerful engine it is possible to make progress to windward even in deteriorating conditions. The combination of power and sail enables the optimum use to be made of favourable tidal conditions, and of course if a harbour has tidal limitations then the availability of a powerful engine can help to meet tidal deadlines – or even those imposed by restaurant or pub closing times! These may be convenience factors for the cruising yachtsman, but the main advantage with the motor sailer is that you have a real alternative if either the engine or the sails fail, so that you can be largely self-sufficient.

The protection offered by the wheelhouse or steering shelter means that the sailing season can be considerably extended without undue discomfort. I have made passages in a motor sailer when temperatures dropped to minus 7°C and we had to break the ice to get out of harbour. Other than needing a good heater, the basic motor sailer was more than adequate for the conditions.

The motor sailer does not, of course, appeal to everyone. Yachtsmen are prone to take up uncompromising positions on the side of either power or sail. The purist who will not touch a motor in any shape or form will certainly not be interested in a motor sailer, nor will the person who wants to race either under sail or under power. Their approach must be one of no compromise in any aspect of the design. The motor sailer does not cater for such stands, but in adopting such attitudes, purists should recognise that they are missing out on some of the best cruising yachts on the market today.

For too long the motor sailer has been seen as a hybrid type of yacht, with bad features resulting from unsatisfactory compromises in the design. Although this may have been true of early designs, production motor sailers now offer much better solutions, and I can see their popularity increasing as the sound and seamanlike qualities of the motor sailer are more widely recognised. The trend is there, and a wide variety of designs is available offering many different approaches to the cruising motor sailer concept. That the motor sailer is now a distinct and respected category of yacht in its own right is beyond dispute, and the fact that it has many enviable features not found in other types of yacht is being realised by an increasing group of discerning owners.

The true motor sailer is a combination of motor and sail aimed at producing the ideal cruising yacht. The design can now offer the best of all possible worlds, and the modern image of the motor sailer is one of quality and reliability. In this book we will explore ways of getting the best out of this unique craft, and look at solutions to any particular problems which may arise.

CHAPTER 2

▬▬

HULL DESIGN AND CONSTRUCTION

Design factors

We have already seen how motor sailer design sits between the some-times conflicting requirements of power and sail. When a designer sets out to produce a motor sailer he has to consider a wide variety of parameters which affect the design. In his design brief he will have been given some idea of the length required, the number of berths required and a broad outline of the characteristics he has to build into the vessel. Existing or past motor sailer designs will also provide ideas. The main objective in developing a design will always be to obtain a harmony and balance between the varying factors which will affect performance, seaworthiness and safety.

Hull design is very much a question of evolution rather than revolu-tion, and from the vast number of different hull shapes which have already been produced there is only limited scope for fresh ideas. The hull of a boat, and particularly a motor sailer, involves a great number of varying and interrelated factors. Many can only be optimised at the expense of others, so that the designer will attempt to produce a hull shape which is the best compromise for the particular purpose for which the boat is intended. With a motor sailer this balance becomes more important because the designer also has to balance the sometimes conflicting requirements of operating under sail and motor. He also has to consider how the boat will behave when power and sail are used in combination, so that developing a motor sailer design requires addi-tional skill and experience. Not only must the hull shape be practical and work efficiently under the different modes of propulsion, but the designer must also consider the aesthetics, which is an important aspect of the appeal of this type of craft.

Construction material

One of the first things which has to be settled in the basic design is the construction material, and here there is still a wide choice. Whilst almost all production motor sailers on the market today are built in glass fibre,

Two alternative motor sailer hulls. The boat on the left is the more sail orientated type with finer lines, which needs 'legs' to stand upright when dried out. The fuller hull lines of the motor orientated type on the right would still need legs, but here twin steel plate bilge keels provide the necessary support.

even with this material there is a wide variety of different construction methods which are possible, and each has its own characteristics and design requirements. Wood construction is still used to a limited extent in motor sailer construction, and this is the traditional material from which all early motor sailers were built, and which to a certain extent was used to determine the hull shape. Those fine sweeping lines which were character-istic of early motor sailers, and the pronounced sheer, were a direct result of using timber construction. In many cases these have been carried over into modern motor sailer designs based on glass fibre hulls, partly because the traditional appearance is still very attractive to many buyers, but also because the hull shapes have been tried and tested over many years and found to be a practical solution to a sound, seaworthy hull design.

With glass fibre construction the designer has much more freedom to make subtle alterations to the hull shapes. As long as the hull comes out of the mould cleanly, and the hull shape is free of hard spots – areas where there are sharp changes of angle, which can lead to weaknesses in the lamination – there are no real limitations in using this material. One of the main benefits of using glass fibre construction, apart from its obvious attraction for building series production designs, is the ability to achieve a very high standard of surface finish and its low maintenance. In the past glass fibre construction was hailed as a 'no maintenance' material, but experience has shown that this is certainly not the case: like other boat building materials it does require a degree of maintenance if it is to have a long and active life; although certainly the maintenance of glass fibre hulls is considerably less than those of other materials.

The majority of production glass fibre motor sailers are constructed from a single skin of glass fibre laid up to a thickness determined by the designer to give adequate strengths. The hull shape with its double curves will impart this single skin of glass fibre with a considerable degree of rigidity, rather like an eggshell, but in most cases additional stiffening is required. This comes in the form of glass fibre ribs inside the hull. These internal ribs or frames do take up some of the internal space inside the hull, and some designs use 'foam sandwich' construction in order to achieve an adequate degree of hull stiffness. With 'foam sandwich' construction there is an inner and outer skin of glass fibre with a layer of foam in between, so that the overall thickness of the laminate is considerably increased: this gives rigidity. To be successful, foam sandwich construction has to be carried out carefully, and there are several proprietary foam materials on the market today specifically designed to meet the requirements. End grain balsa wood has also proved a very successful core material, but whatever material is used, it is important to ensure that there is a strong bond between the inner and outer skins of the laminate in order to prevent delamination, which in turn can lead to cracking and water entering the laminate.

Because foam sandwich construction uses two thinner skins of laminate rather than one thick skin, it can be more vulnerable to impact damage, and consequent water ingress into the laminate. This is one of the reasons why foam sandwich construction is less often used on the areas of the hull below the waterline which would be susceptible to impact damage from floating debris; it tends to be restricted to the topsides which require additional stiffening, and for deck and superstructure panels. One of the main advantages of foam sandwich construction is its good heat and sound insulation properties, which reduces the requirement for additional linings inside the hull.

Ferro-cement is a material which has some of the characteristics of glass fibre construction, but is much more geared to the one-off home construction of motor sailers. Whilst there have been attempts to produce production boats in ferro-cement, these have not proved economically viable, and glass fibre has virtually taken over the whole of the production construction of motor sailers. However, motor sailer designs have a particular appeal to the home builder, and here ferro-cement can be an attractive material because it requires very little in the way of specialist skills and equipment. A steel armature is built up from rods and wire netting to form the basic shape of the hull, and this tightly knit armature is then impregnated with a special mix of cement mortar, which when carefully finished forms the hull. You won't get the same high standard of finish with a ferro-cement hull as you would with a glass fibre hull, unless a great deal of time and effort is spent in filling and polishing the hull, but then the home constructor is less concerned with a high degree of finish and much more with practical construction methods which he can handle in his back yard. Ferro-cement construction can produce a strong and safe hull, provided that the critical mortaring operation is carried out carefully and thoroughly. However, ferro-cement hulls have a very poor second hand value, and are generally not particularly welcomed on the second hand market, largely because it is very difficult to adequately evaluate the standard of construction once the hull has been built.

Metal in the form of steel or aluminium is also used for the construction of motor sailers today, particularly those in the larger sizes, which tend to be one-off designs which do not justify the production of a mould for use in glass fibre construction. The hull is first built up as a framework of ribs and stringers to develop the hull shape; this framework is then coated with the metal plating. It can be a laborious, time-consuming method of construction and, once produced, the hull still needs filling and sanding if a high standard of finish is to be achieved. However, metal construction does lend itself well to one-off designs, provided that the shapes involved are not too complex. Metal is comparatively cheap for hull construction if the metal plates only have to be bent in one direction. Double bends to form more complex hull shapes is a skilled and expensive process, so in most designs tends to be limited to areas around the bow and stern of the hull. Steel tends to be cheaper and stronger, and is probably the favoured material where weight is not critical, but aluminium is easier to work and easier to shape than steel, and so tends to be used for hull construction where the shape is more complex.

Hull designs have been developed for motor sailers on the hard chine principle, where very little in the way of complex plate shaping is required. Single chine hulls have a sharp change of section at the bilge where the top sides meet the bottom of the boat at a hard angle. In order to soften this angle, double or sometimes treble chine construction is used, which still allows plating with only a single curve to be used, but where a series of chines break up the hard angle into a less severe change of section. The same sort of hull construction can be used for wood where plywood is used as the hull plating material. Unlike aluminium or steel, plywood can only be bent in one direction, and although plywood is not a popular boatbuilding material these days – except for the internal fitting out – it is still used on some home construction projects where it is a comparatively simple material to use. Indeed this hull construction by single or multiple chine designs is almost entirely used on home construction projects because it obviates the need for expensive machinery and difficult construction techniques.

There is no doubt though that glass fibre is the main construction material used for motor sailers these days and the flexibility in design which it offers has been largely responsible for most of the major improvements in boat design over the last few years. The refinements in hull shapes which are made possible by using glass fibre construction have enabled designers to optimise hull shapes in order to improve performance under both power and sail, so that less compromise is required in the design to achieve these two often conflicting ends. Today practically all motor sailers under 45 feet in length are constructed in glass fibre, and it is only in the larger sizes of motor sailer, which tend to be custom built, and in those motor sailers designed for home construction, that other materials are used. Glass fibre is now a fully reliable boatbuilding material, and classification societies such as Lloyd's have developed construction requirements and approval systems which allow the buyer to be confident about the quality of the hull that is being purchased. In contrast to sailing yachts, where performance is directly related to the weight of the structure, in motor sailers there is rarely any need to pare down the scantlings of the hull structure in order to reduce weight. The hull shape of motor sailers therefore tends to be based on long experience, and the structure is also sound and sensible and designed for a long life.

Seaworthiness

The prime requirement of any hull which is designed to operate in a seaway is that it should be seaworthy. This may be a fairly obvious statement, but there are designs of both power and sailing yachts on the market today which have limitations with regard to seaworthiness. Seaworthiness is in itself a somewhat vague and ill-defined term: it tends to be judged in relation to other boats, and is a very subjective parameter in boat design because there is no obvious way of measuring it in direct terms. However for the serious cruising man who could well be a motor sailer owner, seaworthiness should cover the ability of the design to cope with the wide variety of sea conditions which may be found in normal cruising, and also to have something in reserve for more extreme conditions. Perhaps just as importantly for cruising, the craft should also have a comfortable motion in a seaway.

There are three main factors which affect seaworthiness: length, shape and strength. The first of these tends to be decided either by the designer's brief or the purchaser's pocket. Strength is not usually a problem because most motor sailer hulls are over-designed in these terms, so that there is a considerable margin of safety here. However, the strength factor is obviously important in terms of seaworthiness, because any failure or potential failure in the hull can create serious difficulties at sea, or limit the conditions in which the boat is operated. A motor sailer is primarily a cruising boat and will be expected to be capable of making extensive passages in open water, provided that the boat is of a reasonable size. Smaller motor sailers will usually be restricted more to coastal operations where shelter is not too far away should conditions deteriorate. However, larger motor sailers, say over 30 feet in length, should be designed and equipped to enable them to survive the sort of severe weather conditions that could be expected when making an open passage of two or three days in length. Here you can be outside the range of accurate weather forecasting, so that deteriorating conditions can be expected. Absolute safety can never be guaranteed at sea, but there should be a reasonable anticipation and ability to cope with severe conditions. Whilst winds of over force 8 are comparatively rare, they do occur on at least a few occasions every year in most sea areas. In these extreme conditions the stresses to which a hull is subjected can depend a great deal on how the craft is handled. Shape may not be particularly critical to the survival of a hull in severe conditions, and a hull designed to operate in force 8 seas should be equally at home in even worse conditions, although in these sort of conditions life is never going to be particularly comfortable or pleasant.

One of the difficulties in designing a hull which has to cope with extreme conditions is firstly to know just what the stresses on the hull are likely to be. Once the designer has some idea of these stresses he is much better able to evaluate the strength requirements of a proposed design. Classification societies such as Lloyd's issue tables of scantlings for various sizes of yacht, and any reputable designer and builder will meet or exceed these scantlings. This is fine when working with wood or metal construction because strength can be quite easily measured, and the quality and construction is there for all to see. With glass fibre the strength of the material of the completed hull shell depends a great deal on how it is laid up. Certainly this is just as important as the material which has been put into the hull construction and there is no easy way of measuring the condition of the completed hull once it has come out of the mould.

Most firms building motor sailers exercise strict quality control of the moulding and lay-up of the hull. Classification society approval of the moulds is one way that the owner can be fairly comfortable that he is getting a good quality hull. To compensate for any inadequacies in the lay-up, and because of the difficulty of knowing exactly what stresses the hull will be subjected to, most motor sailer hulls are considerably over-designed in order to give a reasonable margin of safety. It is very rare to hear of a hull failing these days, and here an intending purchaser has to rely either on the reputation of the yard building the boat, or on the watchful eye of one of the classification societies in order to get a hull which is going to give good performance throughout the years of use.

The third factor which affects seaworthiness is the shape of the hull: this is the one which creates most discussion. Unless the design of the hull is really extreme, then the actual shape of the hull is unlikely to have a direct effect on whether the motor sailer will be capable of surviving extreme conditions. Most motor sailer hulls on the market will be capable of surviving extreme conditions provided nothing else in the boat fails such as the mast and rigging or the engine, or perhaps most importantly the crew. It is in respect of the crew that the shape of the hull can have considerable bearing on survival, because a hull shape which has a relatively easy and comfortable motion will not put the crew under so much stress and will enable them to think rationally and make the right decisions in extreme conditions. The hull shape can have a similar bearing on other aspects of the boat, because there is no doubt that a boat

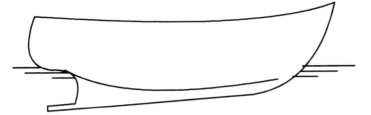

Double-ender with the emphasis on motor performance

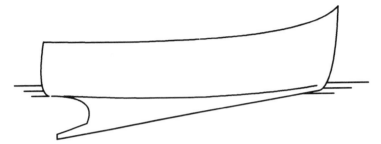

Deep keel hull of the more traditional fishing boat style

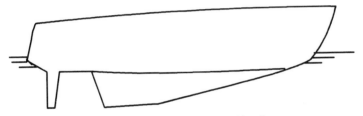

Lighter weight version with separate rudder skeg

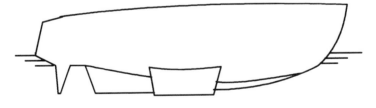

Bilge keel hull with central skeg

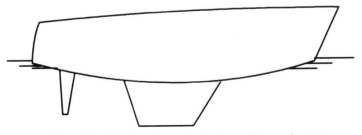

Lightweight hull where the emphasis is on sailing performance

FIG 1   Some of the alternative hull shapes to be found on motor sailers.

which is rolling or pitching very violently will also put undue stress on the mast and rigging and on the engine and its transmission. So in deciding on a hull shape for a motor sailer, we are really looking for a hull which will be comfortable at sea in both moderate and extreme conditions, providing comfort and an easy motion for normal cruising; but also one that does not put the other parts of the boat – or its crew – under very high stress in extreme conditions.

The potential purchaser of a motor sailer should therefore be looking for a hull design which has a comfortable balance and avoids extremes. A fine bow matched to a full stern will not give a boat which is comfortable at sea, as can be seen from watching modern powerboats operating at slow speeds. By the same token you don't want a boat which is narrow in the beam and needs a heavy keel for ballast, because here again you will find a boat which will tend to violent motion at sea, particularly when the sails are not up: this will not be kind to the crew or to the fittings of the boat.

When the boat is going into a head sea or travelling in a following sea it is the shape of the bow and stern which has a major effect on the behaviour of the boat. Whatever shape is chosen it is important that the two ends of the boat balance. If the bow is full then the stern should also be full in shape, otherwise the finer end of the boat will tend to submerge into the waves too readily when the fuller end of the boat rises to a wave. In talking about fullness here, we mean that the hull shape has plenty of volume which in turn gives plenty of buoyancy. If the bow is fine and the stern is full, then the bow will not lift readily in a wave, and the boat will be very wet in a head sea, tending to go through the waves rather than over them. In a following sea the stern will lift readily; once again the bow will tend to go into the waves rather than lift over them, giving not only a wet ride, but also a very uncomfortable one, with an increased risk of broaching. In a following sea, a lot of emphasis is often placed on the shape of the stern being such that it tends to divide the approaching waves rather than offering a large volume of buoyancy to them. Less interest seems to be concentrated on the bow, and yet it is the bow which acts as a fulcrum in following sea conditions when the boat runs down the front of a wave, and if the bow is too deep or too fine it will be immersed in the wave, creating a pivot point around which the stern can swing and broach-to.

The actual shape of the bow in transverse section is not too critical in relation to head or stern seas, provided that there is adequate volume in the sections. Many motor sailers will incorporate a concave shape or flare into the bow shape, so that the buoyancy of the bow will increase rapidly as the hull becomes immersed. This flare in the bow also serves to deflect water away from the hull, thus helping to achieve a drier ride for the boat in a seaway. With most flared bow shapes the lower part of the hull is comparatively narrow, and this fine entry at the waterline means that initially the bow will cut through a wave rather than lift over it, which gives a more comfortable ride and reduces pitching motions. The rapid

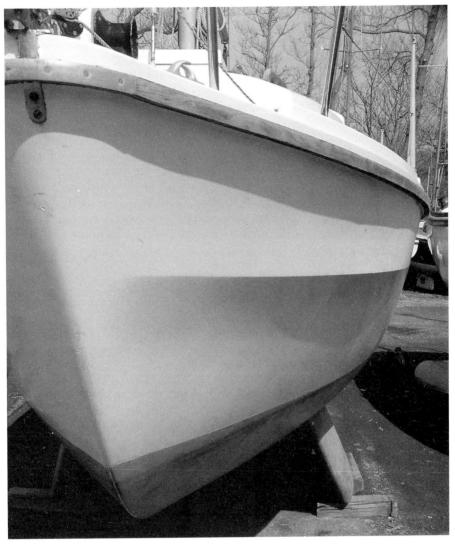

The pronounced 'knuckle' in this motor sailer hull gives fine sections at the waterline while still allowing adequate internal space. It also helps to peel water and spray away from the hull.

increase in the volume of the bow as the flare takes effect will ensure that the bow lifts rather than goes completely through a wave, but will also accelerate the pitching motions when this part of the hull becomes immersed. The concave cross-section in the bow will provide more initial buoyancy, particularly in the lower sections of the hull, but this will not deflect the water away quite so readily. So on many motor sailer designs, a combination of a convex shape for the lower part of the hull, and a concave section in the upper part, is used in an attempt to get the best of both worlds. These bow sections also include a small knuckle

above the waterline. This is incorporated to help peel the water away
from the bow without the need to introduce excessive flare, which is
neither attractive nor particularly practical.

Whilst the stern should have a similar shape to the bow overall, this
does not necessarily mean that the stern should follow the same type of
shape pattern as the bow. The requirements of the stern are different,
partly because this is where the propeller is located, and this has to be
accommodated within the shape, but also because the stern is not
meeting the waves head on. In following sea conditions the waves will
certainly be overtaking the stern, but the period of encounter is comparatively low, allowing time for the passing effect of the wave to be
accommodated more readily. This means that there is less requirement
for fine lines around the waterline, but there is a need for a reasonable
amount of buoyancy so that the stern will lift over waves rather than the
waves falling over the boat. In following seas it is important that the
stern offers as little resistance as possible to waves which may be
overtaking the boat, particularly when these are curling and breaking:
certainly large transom sterns are not a particularly desirable feature,
although it must be remembered that such a stern can be a very practical
feature from the point of view of incorporating a large stern cabin into
the hull.

As far as seaworthiness is concerned, a pointed stern, either of the
canoe or cruiser stern type, is probably the most desirable shape,
reflecting the classic double ender shape which has been well proven in

A double-ended Scandinavian motor sailer with wheel shelter. This can be closed off and the
sliding hatch in the roof used to increase the ventilation options.

terms of excellent seaworthiness. There are still a number of motor sailers on the market today which use this classic shape, but a viable alternative is the truncated counter stern which offers minimum resistance to approaching waves, and also gives a gently increasing lift to the hull as the wave passes underneath. The counter stern can give the motor sailer a finer, leaner look, and tends to be used more in the sailing orientated motor sailers, where this type of stern can give improved performance under sail when the yacht is heeled under pressure of wind.

The transverse cross section shape of the hull, together with the beam of the hull, will tend to have more of an effect on the behaviour of the motor sailer in beam seas, but will also have an influence on the overall comfort and motions of the boat. Most motor sailers in the size ranges up to 45 feet will have a length to beam ratio of about 3:1. A full hull shape with a wide beam is desirable from the point of view of getting maximum space inside the hull to give comfortable accommodation, but such a wide beam also tends to make the boat less efficient from a sailing point of view, so that some of the sailing orientated motor sailers will have a length to beam ratio of 3.5:1. This gives a longer, leaner hull, but such a hull will tend to have quicker motions in a seaway and thus be less comfortable. There is also the question of stability to be considered, and we will look at this in more detail later on, but the narrow hull will tend to require more ballast to give adequate stability, and this will also have a detrimental effect on the motions of the boat in a seaway, particularly when operating under motor alone. The wide beam hull will tend to have more gentle motions and be more comfortable, and this can be an important aspect as regards motor sailer design. The actual shape of the hull cross section can also be important in terms of hull motions: if the bilges are slack, ie the side of the boat runs down to the keel without any sharp angle or curve being introduced at the turn of the bilge, then such a hull will have less stability and be more inclined to roll than a boat with a hard turn at the bilge. Once again it is a question of compromise, since the hull which has a very sharp turn at the bilge can also have sharp motions in a seaway. In general the aim of the designer should be to produce a hull which has no sudden changes in volume or angle in the hull surfaces: this will allow the boat to move smoothly through the water and give a more comfortable ride.

Draft and keel shape

Draft will also have an effect on the hull shape, and on the behaviour of the boat at sea. Obviously a boat with a shallow draft has a lot more scope for cruising in terms of entering small harbours, taking the bottom more comfortably where tidal conditions dictate, and so on. Such a shallow draft can, however, be detrimental to other aspects of the boat's behaviour. In following sea conditions, particularly when crossing a bar where there are breaking waves, then a shallow draft can make life more difficult. In these conditions where a breaking wave is overtaking the boat, the depth of the actual breaking water may be only two or three feet, which can seriously affect a shallow draft boat, because it will be almost totally immersed in this breaking water. A deeper draft boat will have its rudder and a good proportion of the hull still in the more solid water underneath, and this will enable it to maintain steerage way, and greatly reduce the risk of broaching. Even in the open sea a deeper draft motor sailer will be much more comfortable to handle in a following sea because it sits deeper in the water. Such a boat will also tend to have a more comfortable motion at sea because the deeper hull also tends to dampen out rolling movements as the water pressure on the sideways movement of the hull will tend to reduce the effect of the rolling. The shallow draft hull will be much freer to roll, but some designers can reach a compromise here by incorporating bilge keels rather than a deep central keel, and this can help to dampen out the rolling motions as well as providing a satisfactory support for the hull if the boat has to dry out in tidal harbours. A shallow draft hull will also tend to have a much fuller hull shape than a deep draft boat. The change in hull shape can thus be made more gradually, which means that the shallow draft hull in general is likely to be more lively at sea. Draft cannot be treated in isolation any more than beam or the other hull factors, and it is just one of the many parameters that the designer has to take into account. On average, motor sailers between 30 and 60 feet in length tend to have about 1 foot of draft for every 10 feet in hull length, but this is by no means a hard and fast rule, and a great deal will depend on the owner's particular requirements

The powerful lines of a typical motor sailer hull are revealed in this design. The keel is deep enough to give adequate lateral resistance and long enough to give directional stability whilst the generous proportions of the hull allow room for comfortable accommodation.

in terms of cruising and the type of harbours he expects to utilise.

In considering the keel shape we come up against one of the funda-mental differences between motor sailers and other types of yacht. The motor sailer tends to adhere much more to traditional keel forms than other types of modern yachts, be they power or sail. The traditional hull form of a motor sailer has a deep keel with the keel line sloping in a straight line from the bow aft. This is a keel shape developed from the original sailing fishing boats and even from traditional sailing yachts, a shape which has grown out of years of experience and which provides excellent directional stability combined with a comfortable motion at sea. This type of keel is smoothly integrated into the hull shape with no sudden changes in section, which augurs well for a comfortable motion at sea, but is not necessarily one of the most efficient hull shapes as far as sailing is concerned. Whilst there are some motor sailer designs which still follow this traditional line, it has been modified in some more up-to-date designs to have a flatter, more horizontal keel line, which reduces the draft and enables the motor sailer to take the bottom in a more upright fashion rather than lying down by the bow. Such a design would have less directional stability and a smaller aperture for the propeller than traditional designs, but is a good example of the way hull designs have been developed and compromised over the years to meet modern requirements.

From this hull shape we can move on to one which is more sailing orientated in the modern idiom. Here the hull is lighter and has finer lines. It still retains a long keel shape, although this keel – certainly at its after end – is more of a fin keel attached to the hull, rather than an integral part of the hull. With this type of keel the rudder will often be supported on a separate fin and skeg mounted right aft, because the keel itself does not run the full length of the vessel. However, the long straight entry and forefoot are still reminiscent of more traditional hull designs for sailing boats, and this vessel demonstrates the transition to a more modern concept. Now we are coming into the modern sailing boat type of hull, and although hulls of this type are used on motor sailers, they are probably more widely used on sailing yachts, partly because the fin keel means that the engine has to be mounted higher in the hull, where it occupies valuable space which would otherwise be given over to accommodation.

Finally there is the pure sailing boat hull, with a narrow, deep keel which tends to make the boat highly manoeuvrable, but which can lack good directional stability. This latter is a hull form derived primarily from racing sailing boat hull forms, and probably has little place in the repertoire of motor sailer hull forms.

The keel and its shape not only have to be developed to make the hull seaworthy and capable of meeting some of the other requirements of motor sailers, but also has to act to reduce the leeway of the motor sailer when it is under sail, close-hauled. We will look at this in much more depth in Chapter 3 on the forces on a motor sailer, but it is worth noting here that the greater the area of the keel, combined with the underwater sections of the hull, the greater the resistance to leeway, and therefore, to a certain extent, the more efficient the motor sailer will be when under sail alone. Here is another area where the designer has to compromise, and in this case he has to balance the sailing qualities of the hull against the requirements for a shallow draft and for the minimum wetted surface area in order to give the best efficiency when under sail. In some motor sailer designs this compromise is met by using a centreboard or drop keel which can be lowered when the motor sailer is close-hauled or when the wind is on the beam to reduce the leeway, but which can be raised to improve the efficiency when running down wind or when under motor alone. The centreboard or drop keel can be a good compromise when draft needs to be kept to a minimum for entry into shallow harbours, or where the motor sailer has to take the bottom as it dries out at a mooring.

Bilge keels are another option open to the designer, and this is a compromise which is used on many smaller motor sailers. These keep the draft to a minimum, but also allow the boat to sail reasonably effectively. The bilge keels are usually splayed out from the hull at an angle so that when the yacht is heeled under sail, the leeward bilge keel is vertical or near vertical and thus acts as a very effective keel in preventing leeway. These bilge keels can also act as legs to keep it sitting upright when the vessel takes the bottom, whereas single-keeled boats could well heel over in these conditions and make life uncomfortable on board unless stabilising legs are used. In some cases the bilge keels are also combined with a central keel which terminates in the propeller and rudder, although such an arrangement increases the wetted surface of the hull considerably, which would tend to reduce sailing efficiency.

In designing the shape of the keel, consideration has to be given to the location and the water flow to the propeller. A propeller will not work too comfortably behind a big, fat keel, because it does not get a good enough flow of water into the propeller to maintain its efficiency. When we look at machinery and propulsion later on we will see that a large, slow turning propeller is much more efficient than a small, high speed propeller, and the large propeller also helps to keep the boat running smoothly into a head sea in rough conditions because it has much better thrust characteristics. From this it becomes evident that the propeller aperture needs to be as large as is reasonably practical, and whilst the modern trend is towards using small, high-speed propellers which are much easier to accommodate, this traditional approach of a large, low-turning propeller is going to be more effective in rough conditions. Once again the compromise here is between the draft and the propeller efficiency. Since draft is a much more tangible aspect of design, it is likely to receive the priority in this situation, whilst the difference in propeller efficiencies will probably pass unnoticed unless a direct comparison can be made.

One approach to accommodating the engine and propeller is to use a fat, airfoil shaped keel. Such a keel can be fat enough to house the engine, which is then low down in the boat, with the propeller shaft running horizontally to emerge at the rear of the keel. The airfoil shape of the keel helps to keep a good water flow to the propeller despite the width of the keel.

Comfort

The designer must never overlook the comfort aspect of the design, which for most sailers is probably going to be one of the more critical aspects. Most people buy a motor sailer because they want to have enjoyable cruising at sea, and they can only do so if the motor sailer is comfortable; by this I mean in terms of the motion of the boat and the available space on board rather than the use of thick pile carpets and the like. Like seaworthiness, comfort is difficult to define and measure in absolute terms, and one tends to judge comfort by comparing one boat with another or with past experience. It is this same type of comparison which designers use to develop their current designs and again empha- sises the fact that boat design is evolutionary rather than revolutionary. Comfort and seaworthiness are interrelated to a certain degree, but the factors which make for a seaworthy boat do not always make for one which is going to be comfortable.

We have seen how a full bow and stern can make for a seaworthy hull, allowing it to lift over waves rather than go through them. This is fine, but the boat will then want to try and follow faithfully the contours of every wave, and this can result in motions which will be very uncomfort- able. What is required is a bow which will cut partially through the wave and then lift over the wave before that wave buries the bow and sends green water down the deck. This can be a delicate compromise in design simply because there are a wide variety of different sea conditions experienced and the shape of hull that suits one set of conditions is not necessarily good in another set of conditions.

These are the factors which affect the pitching motions, but the designer also has to consider the rolling motions, and these can be more complex in a motor sailer. When the sails are up, they will act as a damper to the rolling motions, but without the sails the rolling generated by a hull shape which relies on heavy ballast could be extremely tiring, with the crew having to hold on continually and being unable to relax. Violent rolling can make life on board very difficult, apart from the very real danger of personal injury which it introduces, but fortunately in a motor sailer you have the means at your disposal to alleviate the motion by using the sails as steadying sails even if you are not using them for propulsion.

When discussing comfort in relation to hull design, space available for accommodation inside the hull also has to be considered. The designer's brief will usually indicate the number of berths that he has to provide and the standard of comfort being sought. While great ingenuity is often shown in making maximum use of available space within the hull, the greater the space the better in many respects, and the designer will always be tempted to make the hull as full as possible in order to maximise the internal space. Here again, a compromise between the internal space requirements and external shape must be reached. One simple way of creating more headroom is to raise the sheer line of the deck. Certainly many modern motor sailers have high top sides in an effort to maximise space within the hull, but this development can often be at the expense of the aesthetic appeal of the hull. This question of appearance can be vitally important. Many yachtsmen will opt for a motor sailer simply because they like the look of the craft and it appeals to their traditional instincts. Most people want their boat to look 'right', and the designer has to anticipate what they will adjudge to be so: the traditional shapes are easily accepted and this is probably why many motor sailers follow these traditional lines. Yachtsmen are basically conservative in their approach to design, and motor sailers probably represent one of the most conservative sectors among the yachting community.

Innovation

We are seeing attempts at innovation in the motor sailer field, and the planing motor sailer and the catamaran come into this category. A planing motor sailer, with all the problems and headaches it creates for the designer, was an attempt to develop a new market for motor sailers, where high speed under power and adequate performance under sail could be combined. The biggest area of compromise had to be in the ballasting of the motor sailer, because weight and speed do not go together, and certainly planing powerboats cannot operate when carrying heavy ballast. Whilst designs of this type have been produced and perform adequately, probably one of the major reasons for the lack of success of this concept is that the aesthetic appeal of these designs was lacking, and combination of what appeared to be a fast powerboat with a tall mast and rigging did not meet the accepted aesthetic criteria of yachtsmen.

The catamaran is a different animal altogether, and here there have been considerable strides in development and performance. The catamaran comes closer to the concept of a planing motor sailer than many people would imagine, largely because the very high inherent stability of the catamaran means that it doesn't need to carry ballast to maintain stability when sailing. Because there is no need to carry ballast, the catamaran is also lighter than a comparable monohull sailing boat, despite its apparent larger size. It can usually sail at higher speeds using a similar sized rig. The catamaran hull with its long, thin twin hulls is also very easily driven and more efficient than an equivalent monohull, and so with only moderate power installed it can achieve reasonable speeds under power. With its twin engines and adequate performance under both sail and power, the catamaran certainly comes within the

There is a large wheelhouse on this motor sailer and extra protection is provided by the spray hood. Note the transom-hung rudder which helps to increase internal space.

category of a motor sailer, although few yachtsmen would accept this, and the catamaran sailor is still generally considered to be the odd-ball of the sailing fraternity, probably reflecting the fact that the catamaran is such a major departure from the traditional concept of sailing boats.

Selection

With the wide variety of motor sailer concepts, and the different approaches to producing the optimum compromise, you may wonder how a motor sailer ever gets designed successfully. Remember too that

The hull of a powerful steel motor sailer. Note the angle at the chine which allows the steel plates of the hull to follow a single curve and simplifies the construction.

we are only considering hull design here, without all the other factors of sail, power and accommodation. However, in most cases motor sailer designs are reasonably successful, and although the compromises that have to be made in designing a motor sailer may be more than with other types of yacht, the end result, judging by the craft on the market today, is certainly an indication of the designers' skills. Most motor sailers today have quite exceptional performance considering the compromises which have to be made. Most motor sailer owners probably put seaworthiness somewhere near the top of their list of priorities, and the generous lines of most motor sailers are evidence of this, but by delicate fining of the lines forward and aft, performance under sail can be maintained. Moderating the draft probably reduces seaworthiness to a certain extent, and again also reduces sailing performance, but these aspects are probably not too significant in a motor sailer, given that the engine is always available to make up lost ground when required – although of course this should not be used as an excuse for introducing poor sailing qualities into the design.

As a result of necessary compromises, there are, on the average motor sailer, only two things which probably suffer to any great extent. Compared to a pure sailing boat the sailing ability of a motor sailer will generally be poorer, particularly when sailing to windward. The accommodation of a motor sailer will also tend to be more restricted than its motor boat counterpart, but there again there is generally adequate space for comfortable cruising, and that is what really matters. There is a tendency in modern designs to start building motor sailers upward to give more accommodation within a given hull length, and whilst the extra accommodation is welcome, the aesthetic appeal of such designs is lower, and this is a trend which will not find acceptance in all quarters.

The choice of hull design for motor sailers on the market today is very wide, and it should be possible for any yachtsman to find one that matches his requirements closely. In today's market, price tends to dictate that the yachtsman opts for a production motor sailer rather than having one custom-built, and so one has to take what is on offer in the market. However, the wide choice certainly offers enough options to enable the buyer to get very close to his ideal motor sailer, and there is no doubt that the larger the craft the fewer the compromises which have to be made. It is probably safe to say that most cruising, sailing yachts over 50 feet come within or very close to the motor sailer category. Here, increased draft is more acceptable on this sort of waterline length, which helps to improve the sailing qualities. The length to beam ratio is reduced, which gives a finer hull shape without sacrificing stability or comfortable accommodation. More efficient and bigger sail plans can be incorporated, and the designer's task becomes much easier.

The hull shape is probably the most critical aspect of the design of a motor sailer, and the use of glass fibre in constructing these yachts has gone a long way to increasing the variety and capability of the hull shapes which are on the market today. The sheer variety of motor sailer designs available does not make the choice of a motor sailer any easier, but in modern designs the compromises have become more compatible and design standards higher, so that the deciding factor for the purchaser could well be purely aesthetic.

CHAPTER 3

▬▬▬

THE FORCES ON A MOTOR SAILER

Although seaworthiness and comfort are, as discussed in Chapter 2, very important considerations in a motor sailer, they are factors which are difficult to quantify. Seaworthiness is a complex matter, but to help give a better understanding of what is involved, we will now look at the various forces which act on the motor sailer when it is at sea. This should help in understanding why the motor sailer behaves in a particular way, and why certain characteristics of behaviour take place.

Speed, lift and resistance

Let us first look at speed, because this is something which is easy to measure and is often seen as a yardstick of performance. The vast majority of motor sailers have displacement hulls. This means that when the boat is moving through the water, the water passes around and under the hull and fills the space created by the hull after it has passed. At all times the hull is supported by its buoyancy: if you think back to Archimedes' Principle, you will remember that a floating object displaces a volume of water equal to its own weight. The weight of the boat acting downwards is balanced by the force of buoyancy acting upwards.

A planing boat, on the other hand, has near horizontal surfaces built into the hull, which are designed to present a slightly angled surface to the water as the boat moves forward. This generates lift under the thrust of the propellers and enables the hull to rise in the water, reducing the effective displacement of the hull because a proportion of the hull weight is supported by the dynamic lift which is generated.

These two means of supporting the hull in the water are important to understand, because they relate to the two main forms of resistance which can affect the hull and thus the speed. It is this resistance to the hull moving through the water which has to be overcome by the thrust generated by the propeller or by the sails. At lower or displacement speeds the main form of resistance is that caused by wavemaking. You can see this in the wake of the yacht. At low speeds the water can flow tidily around the hull and there very little energy is expended in pushing the boat through the water and in generating waves. The faster the boat goes, the steeper and more violent becomes the wake, and the greater the amount of energy which is used to generate these waves. There comes a point where, no matter how much power you apply, the boat will not go faster because the wavemaking resistance is balanced by the thrust from the sails or propeller. A planing boat can overcome this barrier, because the lift generated through forward motion reduces the displacement and hence the wavemaking resistance, and allows the boat to plane.

At higher speeds it is the friction between the water and the hull which is the dominant factor as far as resistance is concerned. Friction between the hull and the water flowing round or under it is present at all speeds, but at slow speeds the friction resistance is small in comparison to the wavemaking resistance. The friction component of resistance rises rapidly as speed increases, and would be a major barrier to higher speeds, except that when a hull starts to plane, the wetted area – that is the surface area of the hull in contact with the water – is reduced as the hull lifts in the water under the dynamic lift induced by forward motion.

With the heavy type of hull found on the vast majority of motor sailers, there is no question of the hull planing, although there may be a small component of lift generated by the forward motion. At the speeds at which a motor sailer travels, the friction resistance is comparatively small, which means that the major component of resistance is the wavemaking resistance. In practice, the displacement hull found on a motor sailer will thus have a hull speed beyond which it cannot be driven no matter how much power is applied. Under sail alone, a motor sailer is unlikely to reach this hull speed, but in most designs it is possible when under power. As the hull speed is approached, the wavemaking resistance rises rapidly, and a great deal of extra power is required for the last half knot or so up to the hull speed. It is uneconomic to operate at or close to the hull maximum speed unless you are desperate to catch a tide. You will also find that easing the throttle will only reduce the speed a little but will give a dramatic reduction in fuel consumption and a notable decrease in motions of the boat and increase in comfort levels.

The main factor affecting hull speed is the length. Whilst on a 25 footer you could find that the hull speed is around 6 knots, a 40 footer could have a hull speed of perhaps 8 knots. There is a direct relationship between the length of the hull and the hull speed, and there is very little that can be done about this. However, a motor sailer which has fine hull lines will tend to have a slightly higher hull maximum speed than a full bodied hull, but the difference is not likely to be more than half a knot unless the fine hull is dramatically narrower. An example of the way the wavemaking resistance can be reduced on a very narrow hull is seen in catamarans. Here the twin hulls are very long and narrow and although the hulls still operate in the displacement mode, speeds of 12 or 15 knots can be possible on a 40 footer. This is one reason for the higher performance found on catamarans, the other main factor being the light weight of the vessel because no ballast has to be carried as the hull is inherently stable.

The wavemaking resistance will change when the motor sailer is heeled over under the influence of the wind. When heeled, the hull tends to present a shape which will increase the wavemaking resistance. At the same time the effective length of the hull can be decreased slightly, both factors contributing to a lowering of the hull maximum speed and the main reason why it is more efficient to sail the yacht as upright as possible. It may look and feel faster with the hull heeled over, but this is mainly an illusion created by the additional waves generated and the excitement of being heeled over.

The effects of the wavemaking resistance will tend to be felt more when under power or in stronger winds when under sail. In lighter winds at low speeds it is the effect of friction resistance which is most likely to influence the performance. The thrust generated by stronger winds or the engine will overcome the friction resistance quite easily, but in light wind conditions you might regret having the added resistance created by the larger surface area of twin bilge keels or a large propeller. With a centreboard motor sailer you can haul the board up to reduce the resistance, about the only step you can take to reduce the frictional resistance on a motor sailer. A fouled bottom will greatly increase the resistance and reduce the lightwind performance.

Stability

Ensuring that there is adequate stability in a motor sailer is the designer's job, but understanding what affects stability can lead to a better understanding of what is going on and enable you to have some control over it. There are many factors which can affect the stability, many of them transient, but let us first look at the motor sailer at rest in calm water.

Here there are two forces acting on the hull: buoyancy, which acts vertically upwards through the centre of buoyancy (CB); and gravity, which acts vertically downwards through the centre of gravity (CG). Both of these forces are individually equal to the weight of the boat, and in still water they are equal and opposite and act through the same vertical line. We can see that the boat doesn't move in still water, and is therefore in equilibrium.

The centre of buoyancy is the geometrical centre of the underwater volume of the boat. Let us first consider the transverse stability, where the centre of buoyancy acts through the geometric centre of the underwater area. The same is true in the longitudinal plane: this will be considered when we look at pitching later. Now, if the boat heels, the shape of the underwater area will change, and the CB will also move to remain at the geometrical centre of the underwater shape. However, assuming that nothing has been moved on the boat, the CG will remain in the same place within the hull, so we find a situation where gravity

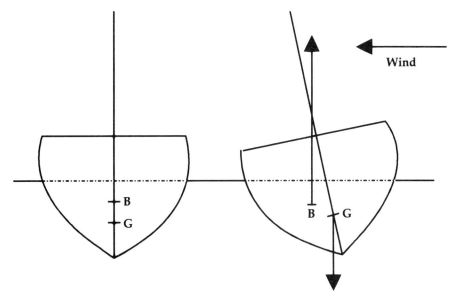

FIG 2   How the position of the centre of buoyancy (B) changes when a motor sailer is heeled by the wind. When B is offset by the heeling it creates a righting moment with B acting upwards and the centre of gravity (G) acting downwards.

acting downwards and buoyancy acting upwards are separated horizontally. The CB will always move to the lower side of the hull, because that is where the underwater area increases when the boat heels, so a righting lever is created by the buoyancy acting upwards and the gravity acting downwards, which wants to bring the boat upright and back into equilibrium.

This inherent stability in the hull will tend to generate a stronger righting force the further the boat heels, which is just the sort of stability characteristic you need for safety. However, there is a limit to the range of stability, because once the boat heels to the point where the edge of the deck becomes immersed, the CB stops moving further outward and may start to move back towards the CG. There is still positive stability at this point, and on most motor sailers this would remain the case right over to 90 degrees or beyond because the CG is kept low in the boat. However, if, when the boat heels, water can find its way into the cockpit or even down below, this could cause a rapid reduction in the stability, because the added weight of the water will tend to move the CG back towards the CB and reduce the righting lever rapidly.

On a motor boat, or a motor sailer under power, the only outside influence which is likely to cause the boat to heel is the effect of waves. Even if the boat doesn't heel, the passing wave will vary the waterline which will change the underwater area. Initially this could mean that the CB moves to the windward side, because the wave has made the hull deeper in the water on this side. With the CG remaining stationary, a moment is generated which will try and heel the boat. This is why a boat rolls in waves. As the wave passes under the boat, the CB moves across the hull to the lee side, and a righting moment is created which brings the boat back upright. In waves the CB is constantly moving from side to side but always brings the boat back upright after the initial roll.

On a sailing boat with the sails up, the heeling effect of the wind in the sails also has to be allowed for. There is, too, the added weight of the mast sails and rigging high up in the vessel: this raises the CG to a certain extent because it will always move towards any added weight. In this situation it is unlikely that the shape of the hull alone can provide adequate stability, which is why ballast is added to lower the centre of gravity and increase the stability.

Ballast can be added in a variety of ways. On pure sailing boats it is generally all put in the keel to improve the sailing qualities and keep the boat as upright as possible for sailing efficiency. The lower down the ballast, the less that needs to be added, because the greater distance of the ballast from the CG, the greater its effect. It would thus seem to be a simple matter to add weight to the bottom of the keel to get the required degree of stability. Certainly there would be no doubt about a motor sailer's stability if that were done, but you would have a very uncomfortable boat: it would become what is termed very stiff. A stiff boat with a low centre of gravity tends to be an uncomfortable boat because it will roll with a very sharp, jerky motion which can be very tiring and unpleasant. With sails up, the wind pressure will help to damp out and moderate the rolling which can produce an acceptable motion on a pure sailing yacht, but a motor sailer has to operate under both power and sail so a more moderate ballast arrangement is usually selected.

Such a system also fits in with the requirement for a reduced draft on a motor sailer to give more flexibility when cruising, and so the required ballast may be shared between the keel proper and internal ballast. The designer will want to reach a comfortable compromise and he will be helped by mounting the engine low in the boat. It is usual to find that the sailing rig on a motor sailer is lower than it would be on a comparable pure sailing boat, so that less ballast may be required to give a safe reserve of stability. The weight of ballast carried on a motor sailer could equal one third of the total weight when a large sail area is carried, but this could reduce to a quarter with a more moderate sail area.

In the fore and aft direction the same situation regarding the relative positions of the CB and CG apply. The difference here is that a small change of angle of pitch promotes a relatively large movement of the CB because of the long shape of the underwater area, so pitching motions are rapidly damped out. As we saw in Chapter 2, the shape of the bow and stern also affects the pitching motions, and at the bow in particular, the increase in buoyancy created by the increase in the bow sections above water can have a major influence on the pitching behaviour. Just as in the transverse situation where too much stability can give an uncomfortable motion to the boat, so too rapid an increase in the buoyancy at the bow or stern can give the motor sailer a violent and uncomfortable pitching motion, particularly in a head sea, where the period of encounter with the waves is more rapid.

As regards transverse stability, there are other factors which can also come into play. When discussing transverse stability we have assumed that the sea surface is reasonably flat. Picture the situation in a beam wind and sea, with the sails set and heeling the boat over, and a wave rising on the windward side. Now the CB will move towards the weather side, reducing the righting lever, so you could find the boat executing a heavy roll to leeward at this stage. This will only be a transient situation, and the rapid change in buoyancy as the wave passes will soon correct the stability, but the heavy roll can make life on board uncomfortable. If the heavy rolling persists then a small alteration of course can often help to give a more comfortable motion by changing the wave encounter pattern.

Another situation which can be potentially more dangerous may occur in a following sea. If the hull remains on the crest of a wave, then the inherent stability could be halved, something to be viewed with concern. This comes about because, with the boat supported by the crest, the waterline amidships is already close to or over the deck level at this point, so there will not be the same corrective force as previously. This situation also occurs in head seas, of course, but when travelling in this direction the passage of the wave past the hull is very quick, and the

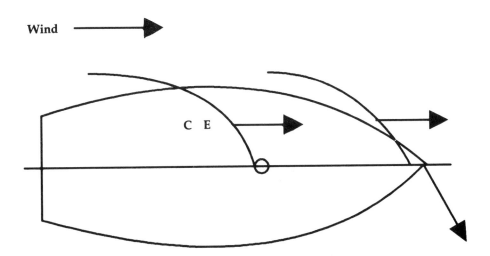

Wind

FIG 3   How the wind acting on the sails when the boat is running before the wind can create a turning effect on the hull. This can be corrected comfortably with the steering, but this effect explains why a boat tends to sheer away from the side on which the sails are set when broaching.

transient loss of stability will pass virtually unnoticed. In a following sea, however, the boat can remain on the crest for a perceptible period, and you could find the boat rolling quite heavily. The chances are that this is likely to be more uncomfortable than dangerous, except that the heavy rolling could lead to gybing. This situation is likely to occur when the boat and wave speed are close and, if you are concerned, then a reduction in speed is the best solution: the waves can then overtake more rapidly which will prevent the motor sailer perching on the wave crest for any length of time.

Stability is a complex subject, and on a motor sailer is made more so because of the need to perform well under both power and sail. The external influence of waves or sudden gusts of wind in the sails can produce instability; you may often find that a small alteration of course or a change in speed can make quite a difference to the wave influence and the motion of the boat. Like everything to do with boats, the stability is related to other aspects of performance.

Centre of effort

Another aspect of performance is related to the keel shape; this will affect the leeway as well as the stability. Ideally what is wanted is a keel profile which will offer maximum resistance to the sideways movement of the hull. With the wind blowing on the sails when reaching or close-hauled there is a fairly strong sideways component to the thrust. This will blow the boat bodily sideways down to leeward, but the hull is shaped to resist this sideways movement, with the keel or centreboard being a major component of this resistance.

For this resistance to sideways movement to be most effective, the centre of effort of the sails should be directly above the centre of lateral resistance of the hull. We will look at this in more detail later in this chapter, but the centre of effort of the sails is the effective point at which the side thrust on the sails can be said to act. If you look at the sails in profile it will be approximately the geometric centre of the sail area. In order to get balance, the centre of effort of the sails should be directly above the centre of lateral resistance, which is the geometric centre of the underwater area of the hull in profile. If the centre of effort is forward of the underwater centre, then there will be a side force generated by the wind which will tend to force the bow downwind. The reverse is true if the centre of effort is aft of the underwater centre. These factors can have a noticeable effect on the steering.

The underwater centre will tend to be reasonably constant in position in a fore and aft direction. It can certainly move upwards when the boat heels in the wind, and whilst this will not affect the steering, it will affect the leeway. The hull offers its maximum resistance to sideways movement when it is vertical. When the boat heels, the draft is reduced and the area offered to reduce leeway is reduced. Not only is it reduced, but the shape of the hull in the heeled condition offers lower resistance to moving sideways, so just at the time when the highest resistance to leeway is needed, the hull resistance can be reduced, another good reason for sailing the yacht as upright as possible.

A bilge keel yacht is better at resisting leeway because one of the splayed keels becomes nearly upright when the boat heels and offers good resistance to leeway. To a certain extent the modern winged keel serves the same purpose, and with this type of keel design the draft tends to remain much more constant to help with the leeway problem. However, both bilge keels and the winged keel offer greater wetted area, and hence greater friction with the passing water. The moral is to try always to sail the boat in as upright a position as possible, which not only offers better comfort, but also helps to reduce leeway. The yacht which has its lee scuppers awash in a strong breeze looks and feels exciting when beating to windward, but it could probably make progress to windward just as quickly under reduced sail and be much more comfortable into the bargain.

We talked about the centre of effort of the sails earlier, and it is worth looking into this in more detail because it can have a significant effect on the behaviour of a motor sailer. The centre of effort of the sails works in two ways. One component is the forward thrust which is generated by the wind on the sails; the other is the sideways thrust, which serves no practical purpose and in many cases reduces the efficiency, as for example when it heels the boat and increases leeway. The problem is that you cannot have one without the other, and the designer and the owner both have to find a balance which optimises the forward component and minimises the effect of the sideways component as far as possible.

This is a complex subject because all the factors are interrelated, but let's look at the sideways component first. If the sails were in a fore and aft line, then the centre of effort of each sail would be at the geometric centre of the sail. However, rather than looking at each sail individually, we are more concerned with the overall effect, so that to find the centre of effort of the total sail plan we have to find the geometric centre of the sail combination. This is the point at which the sideways pressure of the wind will be focused and, in order to get a boat with nicely balanced steering, this should be close above the longitudinal geometric centre of the underwater hull.

However, you cannot make much progress with the sails exactly fore and aft because there is no forward component to the wind thrust. Easing the sheets so that the sails are at an angle to the wind allows the forward component of thrust to take effect. This also reduces the side component but, more importantly, moves the centre of effort of the sails forward because the area of the sails seen in profile has moved forward. This will now change the balance of the steering because the geometric centre of the hull stays in the same place. If the sheets are eased further so that the wind is on the beam, the yacht is reaching and the centre of effort moves even further forward.

So far we have only looked at the relationship between the forces on

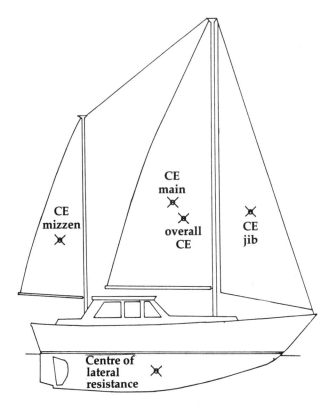

FIG 4 How the individual centres of effort of the sails are combined in an overall centre of effort, which in turn is balanced by the centre of lateral resistance.

the sails and the steering from the effect in profile, ie, the sideways component. However, when the sheets are eased, and particularly when reaching or running, the forward component of the sail thrust is offset out from the centreline of the boat on the side to which the sails are trimmed. This forward thrust will have a turning moment on the hull when it is offset and this will also affect the steering, tending to bring the yacht up into the wind.

It must be appreciated, therefore, that the relationship between the steering, the leeway and the sails is a complex one. The designer will try to assess all these factors and come up with what looks like the best compromise solution, but it will be a compromise and will not suit all conditions. However, when sailing the yacht, the centre of effort can be moved by varying the shape and area of the sails. There are limits with modern sloop rigs because there are only two sails to play with, but by reducing the area of the jib, the centre of effort will move aft, and forward if you reduce the main. One of the joys of the ketch and yawl rigs is the ability to adjust the sail balance to suit the conditions, and whilst there may be less requirement for this on a modern sail boat, on a motor sailer the accent is on comfort: getting the balance of the boat right should be part of this.

This chapter highlights some of the many subtleties in the design of a motor sailer which are required if it is to fulfil its function. The designer tries to achieve a balance so that the yacht will perform well under the wide variety of conditions which will be experienced at sea under both power and sail. Understanding the forces which are at work, adjusting the factors which affect performance, and knowing how to find the right balance to give a comfortable ride, will ensure you get the best out of the design.

CHAPTER 4

▬▬▬

RIGS

What used to be one of the major areas of compromise in motor sailer design, the rig, has benefited from the rapid developments in sail and rig technology in recent years. The fact that a modern motor sailer also has a powerful engine no longer detracts from the sailing performance as it did in the past, as is evident from the fact that what used to be a 50/50 has now become a 90/90. There are still compromises which have to be made in motor sailer rigs, but these now tend to revolve around the size of the mast and sails in the interest of making sail handling and sailing as easy and as automatic as possible. Other compromises also have to be made: the boom is usually set higher to give clearance over the raised wheelhouse, and there is reduced ballast because of the absence of a deep keel. This means that a high aspect ratio rig which features tall masts and narrow sails is less easy to accommodate. However, despite the compromises, most motor sailers today provide enjoyable sailing and the performance under sail is generally more than adequate, although light air sailing is not generally regarded as a feature of motor sailers.

Performance

With the motor sailer rig, squeezing out the last ounce of sailing performance is not generally the requirement. If this is what you are looking for then you should be selecting a high performance sail boat rather than a motor sailer where comfortable cruising is the main requirement. On an average motor sailer, in a fresh breeze, it is usually possible to sail quite close to the maximum speed of the hull, which for a 35 footer would be around 7½ knots. Even if you double the power available, there will hardly be any increase in speed once this maximum has been reached. Racing yachts can spend a lot of time and money in trying to find the extra power from the sails to gain a slight bit of extra speed, but the improvements will be very slight compared with the cost because they are operating close to their maximum hull speed anyway. Lower down the scale, a reduction in the available power by, say, a half, from what is required to achieve the maximum, will still give good performance, and for the 35 foot hull should still give speeds of over 6

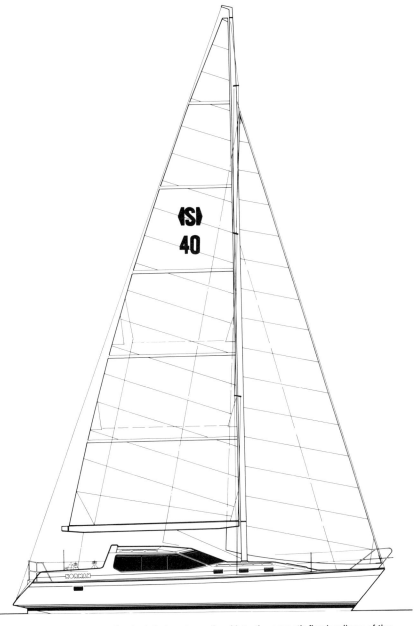

FIG 5 The sailing rig on a sail orientated motor sailer. Note the smooth flowing lines of the integrated wheelhouse and the full width battens in the mainsail.

knots. You can see this from the performance when the vessel is motoring. A considerable reduction in rpm from that giving top speed will have little effect on the performance, provided the boat is generously powered; the speed may drop by only 1 knot whilst giving a good saving in fuel. Sailing at 6 knots in a motor sailer of 35 feet would be considered adequate by most owners, and can be achieved with a fairly simple rig and sails, not too large or heavy for two people to handle. It may be nice to have the extra touch of speed which the hull is capable of, but on a motor sailer this is most easily achieved by turning on the motor if the extra speed is vital. Certainly the complication and extra cost of a larger high performance rig cannot be easily justified on a motor sailer. On a racing yacht every last ounce of speed counts, and the consequences and costs of obtaining these speak for themselves.

Where the rig performance counts much more on a motor sailer is in light winds. This is when you can really start to feel the inadequacies of a smaller rig. The boat will still move but the combination of a heavy hull and relatively small sails is not conducive to light wind performance. The frustration involved will almost certainly mean that most owners will start the engine in these conditions, but then this is what motor sailing is all about, and whilst the sail enthusiast may be unhappy at this attitude, it is essentially a practical one because it allows the rig to be of a size and scope which can easily be managed by a minimum crew. There are some designs of motor sailer where the hull is built to lighter scantlings and which are fitted with an efficient rig for light weather sailing. Here there may be less compromise: motor sailer design is improving all the time, largely with the aim of improving the sailing qualities.

Given that a motor sailer is fitted with a reasonably efficient sailing rig, then the power available from the sails will be more or less proportional to their area. Having determined the power to drive the hull through the water, the designer will then work out the sail area required, but this will in turn depend on the wind strength at which maximum speed is to be obtained. This wind strength for maximum speed should obviously be as low as possible; the sail area can always be reduced if the wind gets stronger. However, the converse is not true, and it is not particularly easy to increase the sail area to improve light wind performance given the limitations of a particular mast height and the desire to avoid complication. The designer of the rig has a complex task: not only does the rig have to produce power over a range of wind strengths but also on all points of sailing.

Balance

In hull design the weight of the vessel is assumed to act through the centre of gravity (CG). With sails, the power produced by the sails is said to act through the centre of effort (CE) of the sails, and the position of the centre of effort will alter both longitudinally and transversely depending on how the sails are set. In working out the stability of the boat in relation to the CG and CE, most calculations will be made with the boat in the close-hauled configuration, because this is where the wind exerts its strongest heeling moment. When close-hauled, only a small proportion of the wind's force is translated into a forward motion, and quite a large proportion is acting on the sails to heel the boat. There must be adequate righting moment both in the transverse shape of the hull and in the ballast located in the hull or in the keel to counteract this heeling moment. To a certain extent the effect of the wind in this transverse heeling is self compensating, because the further the boat heels over, the less will be the effective area of the sails exposed to the wind; the CE will also be effectively lower. If the boat heels over to the point where she is on her beam ends, then there will be no sail area exposed but, hopefully before this stage is reached, there comes a point of equilibrium even in the strongest of winds, where the wind pressure and the righting moments balance each other.

When calculating the position of the centre of effort when the vessel is close-hauled, the first step is to find the centre of effort of each of the sails. In the close-hauled situation with the vessel upright this could reasonably be assumed to be the geometric centre of each sail. This provides two or three individual CEs: the overall CE can then be calculated from the relative positions of these three individual CEs.

When running before the wind there is very little transverse thrust on the sails and consequently very little heeling moment. However, if the wind comes on the quarter or further towards the beam, then the heeling moment will increase, but obviously if there was adequate stability in the close-hauled situation then it will be adequate for these other situations, although it should be borne in mind, as discussed in Chapter 3, that the inherent stability in the hull can be reduced when operating in a following sea, because the boat may be perched on a wave crest for some time which tends to reduce the inherent stability.

The position of the CE is also used to achieve the correct balance on the steering. We have looked at this to a certain extent in Chapter 3, but in this regard we are looking at the individual positions of the CE of each sail rather than the overall CE. The balance of the sails largely determines how a boat steers, and if sailing is to be a pleasurable experience then the balance should be right. We have seen how the sideways thrust of the wind on the sails heels the boat when close-hauled, but this thrust also drives the boat bodily sideways through the water, creating leeway. This leeway is resisted by the underwater portion of the hull which acts through the centre of lateral resistance (CLR). This can be considered to be the geometric centre of the underwater shape of the hull in profile. If the CE of the sails and the CLR of the hull are not above each other, then they will combine to produce a turning force which will tend to steer the boat. Where the CE is forward of the CLR, then the boat's head will turn to leeward, and vice versa. Either way the rudder will have to be held at an angle to compensate for this steering effect which will increase drag. Holding the rudder in this way can prove very tiring for the helmsman and put an unnecessary strain on the steering gear; it can also make efficient sailing difficult. It is almost impossible to get a complete balance, and tends to take the feel out of the steering. Most sailors will prefer a boat which carries a modest degree of weather helm, ie if left to

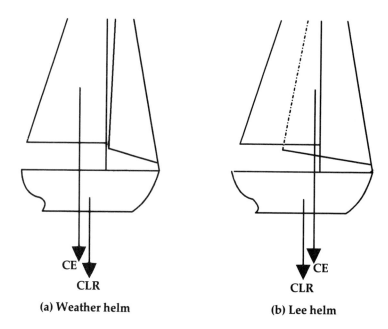

(a) Weather helm　　　　　　　　**(b) Lee helm**

FIG 6　Boat (a) has weather helm where the centre of effort (CE) of the sails is astern of the centre of lateral resistance (CLR) of the hull. In this condition the boat will tend to want to head up into the wind if left to its own devices; most helmsmen prefer this. Lee helm as shown by boat (b) is when the CE is ahead of CLR. When the two are in balance, the steering would be neutral.

its own devices it will round up into the wind, and this is what the designer aims for when determining the shape of the rig. This fail-safe means that if caught out in a sudden squall the boat will round up into the wind.

We have been considering the CE and the CLR in terms of a boat standing upright with the wind blowing directly on the beam. This is not a situation which would occur in practice; in reality, therefore, the correct balance is a much more complex job. There are a number of factors which will affect the CE and the CLR on any given boat, and the angle of the sails to the wind and the angle of heel are just two of these. Suffice it to say, the two centres vary both in their positions in relation to the hull and in their relation to each other. At best their calculation will be an approximation by the designer in his attempts to optimise the two, but it is also possible for the skipper to vary the settings when sailing.

Obviously with a centreboard motor sailer it is possible to change the CLR by raising and lowering the centreboard. This will tend to change its vertical rather than its horizontal position, except in the case of a swing keel, when retracting the keel also varies its longitudinal position to a certain extent, which in turn can affect the steering. Otherwise, the main scope for altering the steering balance lies in trimming the sails. When sailing close-hauled there will not be much scope for this simply because, for sailing efficiency, the sails need to be trimmed to their optimum. In a beam sea, easing the jib sheet will reduce the lateral thrust on this sail and help to move the CE further aft, and setting a smaller jib could have much the same effect. Another option if the boat is badly out of balance is to reef one or other of the sails to reduce their area, thereby changing the balance of the sails, whilst with cutter or ketch rigs there is a lot more scope for changing the balance simply by adding or subtracting sails.

The balance of the sails is vital in a situation where the wind is freshening and you start to put in reefs. In a fresh wind you will be much more conscious of the sail balance, and if you simply reef the main then you are moving the CE of the sails forward which can make the steering very heavy and difficult, possibly changing the weather helm into a lee helm. This emphasises the need to keep the balance of the sails even when reefed down in strong winds.

Sail handling

In designing a motor sailer one of the main aims is to produce a boat which will perform efficiently under most conditions and which can be handled with ease by a minimum crew. Sail handling is probably one of the main tasks to be carried out on board, and obviously the larger the sails the more difficult it can be to handle them comfortably, particularly when the wind is freshening. It is for this reason that we often see motor sailers with their rigs split up into smaller sails, rather than the large main and jib/genoa found on dedicated sail boats. Both ketch and cutter rigs are feasible for motor sailers, but the emphasis tends to be towards the ketch rig in motor sailer design, and this certainly gives a lot more flexibility in finding a rig to suit the conditions, with one of the simplest solutions when the wind freshens being to take down the main and leave the two smaller sails in position. This should still keep a reasonable balance for the sail system. A cutter rig can give a certain amount of flexibility, but generally entails having a bowsprit. This is a feature not found on many sail boats today because of the extra cost in mooring fees, which tend to be based on the overall length including the bowsprit. The cutter rig also makes it less easy to handle the two foresails effectively without someone going up on to the foredeck when changing tack. The cutter rig is commonly used on many of the larger motor sailers of over 60 feet in length, where it can be accommodated without recourse to a bowsprit, but in the smaller sizes of motor sailer the choice is generally between the sloop and ketch rigs.

The ketch rig offers enormous variations in balance and a very logical

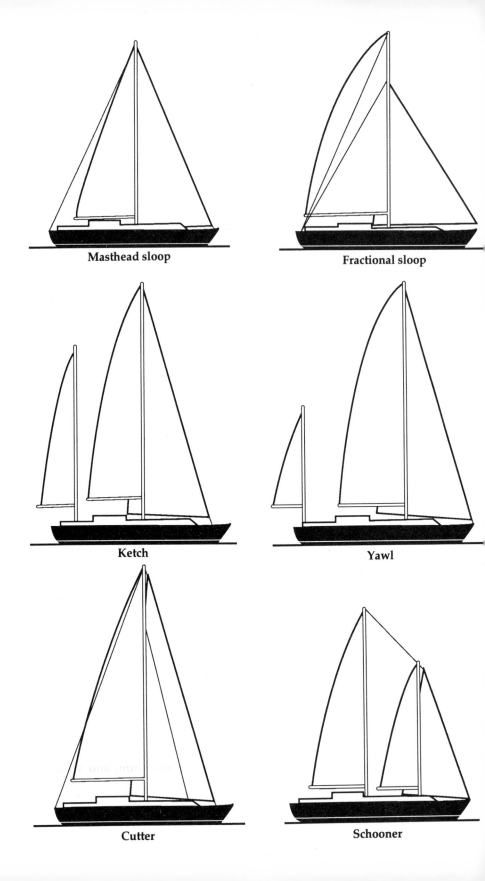

Masthead sloop

Fractional sloop

Ketch

Yawl

Cutter

Schooner

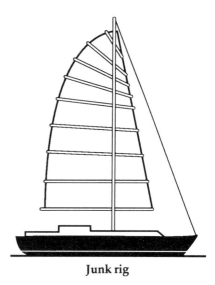

Cat rig

Junk rig

FIG 7   Alternative rigs for motor sailers.

sequence when reducing sail. The mainsail can be reefed without making any significant difference to the balance of the sails, or can be taken in altogether. This means that in a strong wind the larger sail can be taken down and stowed before any really difficult conditions develop in the freshening wind. The remaining sails forward and aft can be balanced easily and are relatively easy to handle if they have to be taken in or reefed. The mizzen is easily handled from the cockpit, whilst most jibs feature roller reefing these days, allowing them to be handled without exposing the crew on the foredeck. The ketch rig also allows the mizzen to be retained as a steadying sail under bad conditions, knowing that it is unlikely to cause any embarrassment. When proceeding under motor, head-to-wind, the mizzen can also be used to help to stabilise the steering and will ease the strain on the helmsman. These features make the ketch rig a very desirable feature for the motor orientated motor sailer.

Steering effect

So far we have tended to look at the forces acting on the sails through the CE as being based along the fore and aft centreline of the boat. This is more or less the case when a boat is close-hauled, but when running before the wind the sails are swung out to one side, and whilst this means that there is very little effect on the transverse balance of the boat, the shifting of the CE from the centreline out towards the side of the boat can have a significant effect on the steering. The boat is effectively being

A powerful ketch-rigged motor sailer with a large genoa to improve light wind performance. The dark edge to the genoa gives ultra-violet protection when it is rolled up.
Photo: Trident Marine

pushed along through the CE of the two sails, and if both of the sails are out to one side, then it is like having a twin screw powerboat with only one engine running. The rudder would have to be put over to compensate for this one sided push and, whilst to a certain extent the uneven pull of the sails might be offset by the extra drag if the boat heels over on this side, there isn't a great deal that can be done to offset this steering imbalance unless the jib can be set on the opposite side to the main as can be done when the wind is directly aft.

Sail wardrobe

The final balancing of any boat under sail is very much a matter of personal preference. The options can be limited when the motor sailer is only fitted with a basic set of sails, particularly where the sloop rig is involved, and whilst many owners are happy to settle for this basic rig, it is possible to introduce a more comprehensive suit of sails which can give more flexibility. The owner really has to decide himself what he wants in the way of sailing from his motor sailer. If he is going to start the engine every time the wind drops to light airs, then there is little point in spending large sums of money on sails. To get a reasonably complete wardrobe of sails could add an additional five per cent to the basic cost of the boat. If the owner intends to spend a lot of time sailing, however, this could be a good investment, and the light wind performance can be increased by adding sails such as a genoa and a spinnaker. Motor sailers which are at the sailing end of the range will tend to come with these optional sails anyway, and if the size of the motor sailer increases then there is an increasing range of options available. One option is a lightweight roller reefing genoa which can be fitted alongside the normal roller reefing jib. Instead of the normal rigid cylinder on which the sail is rolled up, this system uses a flexible wire which is linked to a gypsy type of furling gear. The unit, complete with sail, is hoisted on a normal halyard, and can be taken down and stowed in a sail bag. Even spinnakers today can be handled without the need for poles, which makes them easier to rig and handle, again providing an opportunity to improve light wind performance.

Larger motor sailers will tend to have two masts, giving the option of having a schooner rig and also of setting a staysail between the two masts. If only one sail can be added to the wardrobe, then a genoa is probably the most versatile, as it can be used when both reaching and running. Spinnakers are used on motor sailers, but they do require a degree of expert handling and they certainly don't come in the self-stowing configurations now found on many other types of sail. They do require a spinnaker pole for effective setting and increased halyards, but they are a possible option for light wind sailing.

Alternative rigs

Motor sailers have been the proving ground for some other types of sailing rigs. A tripod mast is one possibility. Although it adds to the weight and windage loft, it does away with the need for the normal fixed rigging. It also gives a more efficient luff to the mainsail because this can be attached to a wire running down to the deck from the masthead. This in turn makes it much easier to install a self-furling main. Another option

A schooner-rigged motor sailer showing the various sail options possible with this rig.

to the conventional rig is the junk rig with its fully battened sail. In true form this comes as a single sail with pole battens, but another version uses airfoil-shaped double battens with twin sailcloth covering, which fit around the mast and effectively produce a wingsail. Both types of sail have been used with free standing masts, although there is scope for introducing rigging to make the structure more robust. Much of the enthusiasm for these particular sails comes from the fact that they are very easily reefed, the battens also acting as the boom at whichever point the sail is reefed down to. These sails tend to be heavier: the fact that they are rarely, if ever, seen on production boats perhaps indicates that they are for the enthusiast rather than for general use.

Reefing and furling

The use of roller reefing and similar systems which help to take much of the hard work out of sail handling has grown dramatically in recent years on motor sailers. Roller reefing jibs are comparatively easy to engineer, and have been around for a long time. Essentially they entail having the

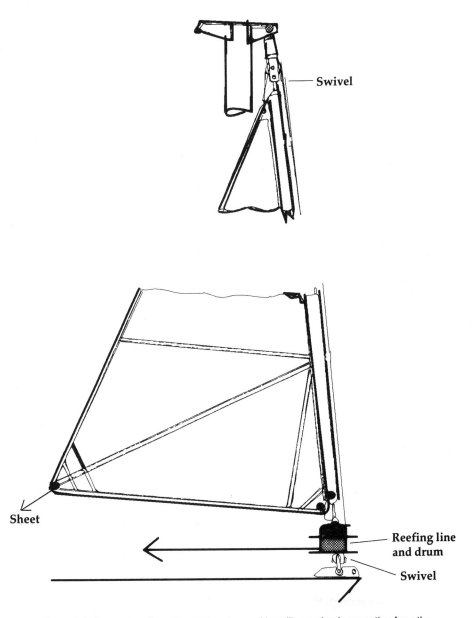

FIG 8   The self-furling system for a jib which makes sail handling a simple operation from the cockpit. The jib is pulled out with the sheet, and the amount unfurled is controlled by the reefing line. To furl the jib the reefing line is pulled, winding the jib in on to its stay.

luff of the jib as a long, narrow drum pivoted at both ends, on to which the sail can be rolled. To furl the sail there are two optional systems, one involving a rope drum where the rope is simply hauled out to turn the drum, which then turns the luff and winds the sail in. This system uses the weight of the wind in the sail and the pull on the sheet to unwind the sail. The second system uses a gypsy and an endless windlass rope to both haul in the sail and unwind it. The roller reefing systems can also be powered electrically or hydraulically; this is a solution often adopted on motor sailers designed for minimum crews.

When applied to the mainsail, roller reefing is less straightforward. One of the most popular methods is to have a roller reefing system similar to that of the jib but enclosed inside the mast, so that the mainsail is then drawn through a luff slot in the mast and rolled up. The tack of the mainsail is attached to a traveller which is hauled out to the end of the boom. Such a system can be operated from a rope driven barrel system fitted inside the bottom of the mast, and certainly provides a tidy solution, although it doesn't allow battens to be put into the mainsail to help enhance its shape. Alternatively the roller system can be located behind the mast rather than inside it. This system might be fitted as a retrofit, but is equally suitable for fitting as original equipment, and at least with such a system you can see what is going on. It does generate extra windage, though, and makes the sail slightly less efficient because of the interrupted air flow over the sail. If a rope winding drum similar to that used on the jib is to be used, it has to be tall and narrow because of the limited space available; it is usual to use a grooved drum so that the rope does not build up and expand over the diameter of the drum. However, a tall, narrow drum does reduce the leverage available, and an option is to mount the winding drum horizontally and use a bevel gear drive.

Another alternative is to wind the mainsail into the boom rather than into the mast. This is an extension of the familiar roller reefing gear which has been in use for many years. Rolled in this way the sail is much more bulky on the roller, but the roller can be the boom itself, or a roller fitted inside the boom. As with mast mounted furling systems, boom furling will not accommodate the normal type of angled sail battens, but a new development is the use of full-width horizontal battens of a round GRP extrusion. Because they are horizontal, these battens do allow the sail to be wound completely on to or into the boom, and have the added advantage of preventing the sail flapping when headed into wind, as could be the case when motor sailing.

Boom furling systems can have the winding drum at the outer end of the boom, where there is more space for it, but the winding rope is led to the inner end of the boom, then down to the deck, and then to the cockpit. Other options are to have the winding drum on the opposite side of the mast to the boom gooseneck, with the drive taken through the mast; or to have a bevel drive with the drum under the boom. A further system uses the same type of tall, narrow grooved drum used with mast

A mast roller reefing system which makes a very tidy job of stowing the sail.

furling, and this is contained within the boom. It is usual with this method to use low friction mast carriages so that the sail comes down cleanly. With all these systems, hydraulic or electrical power assistance can be fitted, and in this way sail handling can be largely automated.

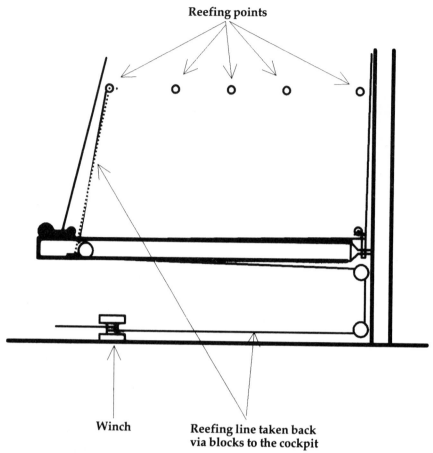

Reefing points

Winch

**Reefing line taken back
via blocks to the cockpit**

FIG 9   A mainsail reefing system where pulling down on the reefing line and slacking the halyard allows the sail area to be reduced. Although the basic operation can be carried out from the cockpit, there is still a need to tie down the excess sail on to the boom through the reefing points.

They can also be complemented by electrically powered winches of the self-tailing type. Powered winches allow the sail to be trimmed at the press of a button, although if you are going to sail in this convenient fashion you have to be aware of the drain on the battery, unless there is a generator running.

As far as jibs are concerned, these roller reefing systems offer a great deal to the motor sailer owner. They make reefing simple and easy and also simplify sail stowage when coming into harbour. They avoid the need to go out on to the foredeck, and everything can be handled from the cockpit: it is just a matter of pulling on a rope. For the mainsail there are more complex mechanisms and a larger sail area involved, which can create problems. But for motor sailer owners not looking for the highest in performance under sail, the advantages can certainly outweigh the disadvantages, and with a two-person crew on a 40 footer, these sail handling systems can make life on board much more pleasant, particularly in stronger winds when the minimum crew could find themselves stretched to handle a large mainsail.

Rigging

The mast is an essential part of the motor sailer rig. Today, masts on motor sailers are almost invariably constructed from anodised aluminium, a material which is both light and practical. In cross section most motor sailer masts are oval, with the main sail track on the trailing edge. The masthead is rigged with sheaves which allow the halyards to be brought down inside the mast to reduce windage and give a cleaner appearance. The inside of the mast is usually sound-deadened with the application of foam or plastic to prevent the halyards making a noise when they tap against the metal and to reduce drumming. The mast will also accommodate the wiring for the masthead light, for the wind instruments, and for any antennae fitted in this area. These will be run down in a conduit fixed inside the mast. If the mast also has to accommodate a furling main, then it gets pretty crowded inside, although the need for halyards is reduced.

Today most masts are stepped on deck rather than in the traditional place in the keel. This avoids the need to cut a hole in the coachroof which can be a potential source of leaks. The various halyards and wires which run up inside the mast are brought out to deck blocks at the base

The clean lines of a modern performance motor sailer. Note the full length horizontal battens which allow for boom roller stowage. They also reduce sail slatting when motoring head-to-wind. *Photo: Van De Stadt*

of the mast, from which the halyards are led aft so that everything can be handled from the cockpit. On modern motor sailers even sail hoisting and lowering can be handled from the cockpit, although you still have to go out on deck to release the sail ties.

Like most other things on a motor sailer, the rigging for the mast has to be carefully balanced to take the multitude of strains to which the mast is subjected. In keeping with the general requirement for simplicity on a motor sailer, the rigging is kept fairly straightforward, and usually only entails the use of a single spreader to help take up the sideways stresses on the mast. Getting the correct balance in the rigging in order to support the mast properly is a delicate art, but the general idea should be to maintain the support and balance of both the lower and upper shrouds, so that the stresses on the mast are evenly distributed. The forestay and backstay should be similarly balanced, because the mast is a fairly fragile fitting unless all the supporting wires and stays are carefully tensioned to spread the load.

Masts and rigging on motor sailers need to be properly designed, and are usually more than adequately robust for the job. Unlike a pure sailing boat where these fittings tend to be reduced to a minimum in the interests of efficiency, on a motor sailer there is scope for making these fittings of adequate strength, reducing the risk of failure. With strong masts and rigging and with modern synthetic sails capable of taking high stresses, the principal limiting factor on the rig tends to be the angle of heel which the boat assumes under the influence of the wind. It doesn't pay to introduce a high angle of heel, because leeway becomes excessive and comfort on board deteriorates rapidly. Even if the conditions suggest that it is better to switch on the engine rather than keep the sail up in strong winds, keeping a minimum of sail up can be useful to reduce the rolling, and the steadying effect of the sails can make life on board much more comfortable.

With modern materials – rigging generally in stainless steel, masts in aluminium, and sails in synthetic fibres – there is little risk of corrosion in the mast and rigging. The main problem is likely to be wear and tear, and this applies particularly to the sails unless you handle them carefully. Even when stowed, a sail can be subject to wear from the ties and from rubbing against metal fittings, and this should be watched if you want to get a long life from your sails. One of the problems with modern synthetic sails is that the stitching does not sink into the fabric, but remains proud, and is thus subject to more wear and tear than the sail fabric itself. This can be the case particularly when running before the wind, when the sails rub against the mast spreaders or the rigging. On long passages they should be checked regularly, and covering provided for any localised wear areas. Wear can also occur through constant movement in the fittings of both the running and the standing rigging, and part of the annual overhaul should be to inspect carefully all the shackles and turnbuckles, particularly on the inside bearing edges which cannot normally be seen, in order to detect any signs of wear so that these items can be replaced before they fail. The wear and tear on the rigging is a slow and insidious process, and it is important to be aware of any damage before it reaches serious proportions.

The mast, rigging and sails of a motor sailer are its power house, and its safeguard against engine failure. Modern systems make for both reliability and ease of use. Knowing how the sails work and how they balance – and their relationship to the hull and the rigging – is vital if you want to get the best out of your motor sailer. Above all, getting the balance right will make a great difference to the pleasure of your motor sailing.

CHAPTER 5

────

HANDLING A MOTOR SAILER

The unique characteristics of most motor sailers introduce unique handling features. An obvious one is the combined use of engines and sails when the boat is 'motor sailing', but there are also many more subtle features which are unique to this breed of boat. A much more positive approach to manoeuvring in harbour can be taken using the powerful engine on a motor sailer when compared to handling a sailing yacht in similar circumstances. Out at sea, the low aspect ratio of the sails, and the generally greater flexibility in adapting the sail area to the conditions, has to be appreciated when under sail, whilst with the same vessel under power a totally different set of handling characteristics has to be taken into account.

Getting the best out of a motor sailer in terms of handling is largely a question of understanding the various forces which operate on the boat as shown in Chapters 3 and 4, but also in achieving a balance of these forces to match the different operating conditions. This sort of balance is one which an experienced seaman will find instinctively, matching the vessel and its behaviour to the sea and wind conditions so that the vessel behaves largely as he wants it to. Novices can achieve similar results by working things out from basic principles until they too eventually become experts. Of course even experts can get caught out on occasion by making the wrong assessment, but the more experienced sailor will usually have something up his sleeve to find a way out of the predicament. With a motor sailer there is probably more scope, more variables incorporated in the design to adapt the handling and performance to the conditions than with any other category of craft.

In looking at motor sailer handling, the subject can be conveniently divided into two categories. The first is calm water manoeuvring, which usually entails the close quarters manoeuvring found in harbours and marinas; the second is open sea work. There are also, of course, the obvious divisions of handling under power, under sail, and using both power and sail at the same time, but the conditions in which you have to do the handling are what really matter. In harbour, the presence of solid objects close by demands more precise handling skills which have to take into account wind, tides and current, whereas out at sea the handling is mainly judged in terms of the effect of the wind and waves on the yacht. With two very viable alternative means of propulsion on the motor sailer, there is a lot that the experienced owner can do to match the conditions.

Harbour handling

In harbour the main influences on the hull will be the wind forces acting on the areas above water, and the resistance to the hull moving through the water combined with the tide or current effects found in the harbour. The effect of the wind will vary with its strength, and with the boat's angle or aspect to the wind. When head-to-wind the effect will be simply to slow the boat down, and the force acting on the hull will be symmetrical on both sides. However, this balance can be tenuous, particularly if there is a high bow on the vessel, or if there is a headsail still up or the sail is poorly stowed. In this situation, if there is a very slight sheer off the wind to one side or the other, then the wind will quickly upset the balance and the wind force will rapidly increase the sheer away from the desired line. This effect will be emphasised at the sort of creep speeds which are often used in harbour.

From a steering point of view, a boat with a lot of windage forward is going to be directionally unstable, particularly when operating at low speeds. Once the wind starts to swing the boat away from the desired heading, then at very low speeds there might not be enough steering force to bring the boat back head-to-wind. If the windage is aft, which can occur if there is a large wheelhouse aft, or if the mizzen sail is still up, then, when the boat sheers, this will expose this area to the wind, tending to make the boat swing back up into the wind and thus give good directional stability even at very low speeds.

The sliding wheelhouse hatch on this motor sailer allows good visibility for harbour manoeuvring as well as ventilation in warm weather.

The same tends to apply to the underwater parts of the hull. Where the hull has a deep forefoot this will tend to accentuate any sheer to the side when the boat is moving ahead. When the underwater area is concentrated aft, the boat will be much more directionally stable when moving ahead. Whilst these above and underwater areas have been considered separately here, in practice they work together, and it is the resulting balance which will affect the boat's behaviour in harbour. It should be borne in mind that the effect of the wind on the steering will be accentuated at low speed because the corrective effect of the rudder is greatly reduced in this situation.

If the wind is on the beam in harbour, then the boat will be blown bodily sideways under the pressure of the wind on the above water surfaces. However, if there is a larger area exposed to the wind forward, then the bow will blow off downwind. Similarly, if there is a larger area aft, then the stern will blow off downwind. Once again, though, these effects must also be related to the underwater hull shape. With the stern generally much deeper in the water, there is more resistance to sideways movement in this area than at the bow, which will thus tend to blow off under the effect of the wind much more readily. Here we come back to much the same situation which was discussed in Chapter 4. Although there are no sails in this example, the centre of lateral resistance still acts as the focus for resistance to sideways movement and the areas of the boat exposed to the wind, and will act through the centre of effort; a simple calculation will enable you to work out what the effects of a beam wind will be when the boat is operating at low speeds without the sails.

The effect of this balance is likely to be particularly significant when you are coming alongside with the wind on the beam, because it will become more pronounced as the boat loses way through the water, and any tendency for the bow to swing off the wind is more difficult to correct with the rudder. It can be embarrassing when having completed a nicely judged run-in alongside to find that the bow of the boat suddenly seems to be taking charge and swinging uncontrollably, but what is really happening is that the rudder is losing its steering effect and the wind is taking over.

A wind from astern will not only increase the speed of the boat but could affect the steering in a similar way as when the wind is ahead. With the wind astern, the boat is less likely to be directionally stable, because most motor sailers are designed to be directionally stable going into a head wind.

Propeller effect

When travelling at slow speed in harbour, the motor sailer tends to behave in a similar fashion to the traditional power craft. Unfortunately, few yachtsmen have experience with this type of craft, because the modern power boat is a lightweight craft, often with twin screws, which has little grip on the water and is greatly affected by the wind because of the high topsides. Compared to this type of craft the motor sailer can be a treat to handle despite having only a single propeller.

With a single screw vessel, it is not always easy to counteract this wind-induced swinging when operating at very low speeds. If you open the throttle to try and get a stronger steering effect on the rudder, then the boat will be moving ahead through the water just at a time when you probably don't want it to. However, with most motor sailer designs there is a way of achieving a steering thrust without giving the boat any headway. This is done by first of all putting the rudder hard over in the appropriate direction, and then giving a sharp burst on the throttle – probably just for a second or two. With the rudder hard over at an angle of about 30 degrees, a great deal of the thrust from the propeller will be directed sideways to give steering effect, and a quick burst on the throttle will not be enough to give the heavy hull the chance to gain any ahead momentum, so that in effect you have an action almost like a thruster at the stern; this can be used to very good effect when manoeuvring in tight quarters.

The amount of this sideways thrust or 'kick' will vary both with the size of the propeller, its depth below the water, and the relative positions of the propeller and rudder. On motor sailers, where the propeller size is usually fairly generous, where it is located reasonably deep and directly in front of the rudder, and where a balanced rudder is fitted, then the effect of this propeller thrust can be very noticeable and, if used intelligently, can greatly improve the handling of the boat. It is worth repeating that before opening the throttle the rudder should be put hard over, because if you open the throttle first, there will be a strong ahead component to the thrust before the rudder starts to exert its sideways thrust. With a balanced rudder the sideways thrust effect will be more noticeable, because the rudder will effectively block the propeller thrust from running directly astern when it is hard over.

To complicate the situation there is also a sideways component involved in propeller thrust anyway, and this tends to be particularly noticeable at slow speeds when the rudder is less able to correct it. With the angled blades of a propeller there is always a sideways thrust component present on each blade, in addition to the main thrust astern. When the propeller is deeply immersed this sideways component is balanced between the top and bottom blades and has virtually no effect. The sideways component becomes noticeable when the propeller is closer to the surface. The bottom blade is then operating in more 'solid' water than the top blade, where the resistance to the blade can be reduced because of air drawn down from the surface, and therefore less thrust is generated. This means that the sideways thrust generated by the propeller blades does not balance out, and the resultant force can act on the stern as a sideways thrust. With a right-handed propeller, which is the type most commonly fitted to motor sailers, the bow will swing to port when going ahead and to starboard when going astern.

The extent of this turning effect of the propeller can be found by putting the engine ahead in calm conditions with the rudder amidships: you can soon see which way the boat will swing. This pronounced steering effect can be used to advantage in close quarters manoeuvring. For instance, if you have to turn the boat round in a narrow river, then you will choose to swing in the direction in which the propeller thrust will assist the manoeuvre, which in most cases means putting the rudder hard over to port to make the turn. If you have to back and fill to complete the turn then much of this additional sideways thrust will be balanced out, but if you understand what is going on then you can take advantage of the phenomenon.

Although it is customary to put the engine astern to take the way off the vessel as she comes alongside, this sideways component could cause the boat to swing just at a time when you don't need it. When going astern in this way the rudder will have virtually no effect, because there is no stern way on the vessel. If you are faced with this situation, take the way off the vessel by going astern, and then put the rudder hard over away from the berth and give a quick kick ahead on the engine to bring the stern alongside.

Effect of tide

So far we have only talked about the wind and its effect, but the effect of tidal current can also be very noticeable in many harbours and marinas, with the body of water in the harbour actually moving. The problems with the tide tend to be more in respect of navigation than boat handling because this tidal current can in fact make it much easier to handle the boat. In tidal waters you can hold the boat virtually stationary in relation to the sea bed whilst the boat is steaming slowly ahead, and you have full steering control. This allows you to come alongside a berth, providing it is lined up with the tidal flow of course, whilst retaining steering control all the time. This can be particularly useful when picking up a mooring, although you do need to be careful that you do not put on too much helm in this situation, otherwise the boat can get right across the tide when it will drift bodily sideways downstream and you will have to round up and start the mooring procedure all over again. Once again in this situation, it is the quick kick on the engine which gives a good steering effect and can enable you to hold the vessel in just the position you want it to be.

This ability to stem the tide can be particularly useful when entering a harbour in poor visibility. If you do this on the ebb tide, then if necessary you can always stop and work out where you are or what is going on without actually making headway. It enables you to keep control of the vessel, and to maintain a steady heading which helps to keep the radar picture stable.

No two boats are quite the same when it comes to handling, and if you are going to be successful at close quarters manoeuvring in harbour under varying conditions of wind and tide, then there is no substitute for practice. Practising at a buoy or a deserted quay is a good way to gain confidence. One of the things you will need to bear in mind in all close quarters manoeuvring is that a motor sailer tends to be a heavy boat for its size, which means that it will carry a lot of way after the engine is taken out of gear. When the propeller is not turning in this situation you will get less steering effect, but the 'kick' is always available when you need it. Similarly it will take a fair time to pick up speed when the gear is engaged, so that a degree of anticipation is required in any manoeuvring. The astern power is usually very good, which means that you have good brakes if things do go wrong, but it is always a wise precaution when coming in from sea to check that the astern gear is actually working before you get involved in any tricky manoeuvres at close quarters.

Harbour handling under sail

Bringing a motor sailer into a berth or up to a mooring under sail alone can be rewarding, and it should be possible to achieve this in most motor sailers. It is not something which is particularly recommended if you have the easy option of the engine available, and the two main points to remember are the lack of any brakes when you are under sail alone, and the reduced effect of the steering at slow speeds because there is no propeller thrust going past the rudder. You will also need a reasonable amount of wind if the manoeuvre is going to be successful, particularly if there are strong tides around, and you will also need to take into account the shielding or reflecting effect of large buildings which could affect the wind. The lack of brakes and the heavy weight of the boat mean that the

Powering through a tidal race which makes a sea of short steep waves. As a sound, safe cruising yacht, the motor sailer needs to be able to cope with a wide variety of sea conditions.

final approach must be at slow speed and, as far as you can arrange it, with the wind coming from ahead, in order to slow the boat as it comes alongside. You can help the slow speed steering by manipulating the sails, and here a ketch or rig with the sails located at each end of the boat can be very good. Spilling the wind from the jib or the mizzen when the wind is on the beam can produce a considerable steering effect to help the rudder. When the wind is ahead, perhaps when making the final approach to berth, steering can be assisted by backing the jib to one side or the other to help the bow turn.

Whether you are manoeuvring in harbour under power or under sail, the important thing is to get to know your boat. Knowing what it will or won't do under various circumstances can help you enormously when planning a manoeuvre alongside, or attempting to leave a difficult berth. Practice is the main criterion for successful manoeuvring, but it can also help to have an efficient crew, particularly when using the sails or getting a line to the shore when tying up. It is quite feasible to take a motor sailer in or out of harbour singlehanded if you plan things carefully and try to anticipate any problems and requirements beforehand.

Speed and comfort at sea

When handling a motor sailer at sea, the boat should be driven to suit the conditions. By and large, comfort will usually dictate this. If the boat is being thrown around uncomfortably, the crew will probably start complaining. The strain on most parts of a boat also increases as the speed increases, so the boat will not be happy either, though provided you have maintained the boat to good standards, the crew are much more likely to be the first to complain. You should be able to feel when the boat is being over-stressed, either by being driven too hard into a head sea under power, or when heeling over too far under sail. Motor sailing is generally about comfort, and any violent movements of the boat should be taken as a warning.

On the average motor sailer, full speed in a force 4 wind should not create much discomfort, except perhaps in a head sea when the pitching could become a bit violent. You will only be going into a head sea under motor, and in this situation a small reduction in the engine revs should make life on board much more comfortable. It will also reduce the spray being thrown up. As mentioned in Chapter 3, most motor sailers generally have excessive engine power for fine weather work, and the top end of the rpm engine range tends to increase the fuel consumption whilst producing very little increase in speed. In these head sea conditions when the boat is being forced along at maximum power, it will have less resilience when meeting a wave and will tend to force its way through the wave, which in turn can produce an uncomfortable pitching motion and make life on board quite uncomfortable. Reducing the rpm will reduce the pressure on the boat and crew and allow the hull to yield more kindly to the waves, giving a much easier ride.

In beam and following seas under power, this situation will not normally arise in moderate sea conditions, although life on board can become uncomfortable due to excessive rolling. The rolling can be controlled and reduced by hoisting a sail as a steadying sail, and this can be supplemented by a small alteration of course. It is quite surprising how a small alteration of only 5 or 10 degrees can make quite a difference to the motion of the boat and the way it performs in waves. Much of the discomfort at sea on a motor sailer under power can be due to insisting on steering direct to your destination, rather than adopting a more flexible and comfortable course.

When operating a motor sailer under sail, the motion will tend to be

Full sail in a strong wind, demonstrating how the small sail area of some motor sailers reduces the need for sail change when the wind freshens.

much more comfortable. In these conditions the pressure of the wind acting on the sails tends to modify the motion of the boat and act as a damper against the wave-induced motions which cause discomfort. A good, strong motor sailer, particularly one of the motor orientated type, will be able to carry full sail up to about force 5 without much of a problem, but if you carry full sail in a freshening wind, then you will probably find that although the boat is not going much faster, life on board is becoming more uncomfortable. Reducing sail in these circumstances will greatly reduce the stresses on the mast rigging and hull and will make life on board more comfortable because the angle of heel will be less. As with running under engine, the speed will only be reduced by a fraction. With a motor sailer there is very little point in trying to squeeze out the last ounce of speed in any conditions, because the hull tends to be designed more for comfort than for speed. You can still sail efficiently, but that is very different to sailing at maximum speed.

Sail and engine

It is quite likely that a motor sailer at sea is going to spend quite a lot of its time operating with both the engine running and the sails up, particularly if it is working to some sort of schedule. Whilst the engine enables the speed to be maintained, the thrust generated by the sails assists, reducing fuel consumption and allowing the engine to be run at a lower rpm for a given speed. Having the sails up also tends to make the motion more comfortable; operating with this combination of engine and sails is one of the features of motor sailer life which makes a very viable cruising combination.

However, running under engines and sail does affect the way the sails perform because of the apparent wind generated by the engine thrust. The apparent wind is the wind that you actually feel on board the motor sailer, and the strength and direction of the apparent wind is a combination of the true wind, ie the wind which you would feel if the motor sailer was stopped at sea, and the wind generated by the movement of the boat through the water. You get an apparent wind even when under sail alone, because the boat is moving ahead and generating a wind effect from its speed as far as the sails are concerned. On a motor sailer this effect will be accentuated when the engine is being used because of the increased speed of the boat.

The apparent wind will be that measured by the wind instruments. It will always be forward of the true wind, which means that you will need to sheet the sails in harder when the engine is being used. The speed of the apparent wind will always be greater when sailing close-hauled, and less when the wind is aft. Finally, the angular difference in the directions of the true and apparent winds will be greatest when reaching. These factors will become clear from a study of the diagrams.

In general the sails will be less effective when the engine is being used. For instance, the boat will not be able to point up so closely into the wind

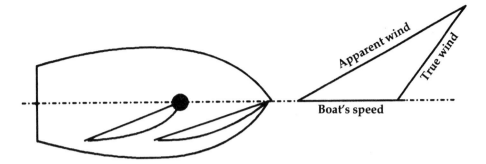

FIG 10   The correlation between the apparent and true wind. The true wind will remain the same for given conditions, whilst the apparent wind direction will vary with boat speed.

when the engine is running, because the apparent wind will have moved further forward. When the wind is aft, the forward speed of the boat under engine will effectively reduce the wind strength. In light winds the difference between the apparent wind and the true wind will be much more noticeable, because the wind generated by the forward movement created by the engine thrust will be stronger in relation to the true wind. As wind strength increases, so the difference between the true wind and the apparent wind becomes less. In terms of motor sailing, this means that if the true wind is within 60 degrees on each bow, then it is unlikely that the motor sailer will be able to sail close-hauled when the engine is running as well. It is in beam winds that the sails can be most effective when used in conjunction with the engine; in this direction the sails also have a good steadying influence on the rolling of the boat, so beam winds and the engine running is a happy combination for the motor sailer. Of course there is nothing to stop you altering course 10 or 20 degrees to allow the sails to be more effective when using a combination of motor and sail.

With a powerful engine always readily available, less attention is often placed on getting the sailing rig on the motor sailer working fully effectively. This is a somewhat negative approach, bearing in mind that the more efficient the rig, and the closer the yacht can sail into the wind, then the greater the range over which motor and sail can be used in combination. Under sail alone a motor sailer should be able to sail to within 45, perhaps – with a very efficient design – even 40 degrees of the wind. Efficient sailing is certainly going to extend the range over which the motor can be used in conjunction with the sails.

Heavy weather

With the motor sailer projected as a very effective cruising vessel, then inevitably it will be faced with operating in less than ideal conditions. Unless the motion of the boat tells you first, the initial sign that conditions are starting to deteriorate will be when spray starts coming aboard, and perhaps even when the occasional sea is shipped on deck. Certainly when solid water starts to come on board it is time to think about easing back, or finding a more comfortable heading, because solid water brings with it the risk of damage. In such conditions the prudent seaman is going to start looking at the options which are open to him. In a motor sailer there are plenty of these available, but in order to make sensible decisions, one of the first steps is to get an accurate weather forecast on which to base any future decisions. Don't take the weather forecast you obtain as gospel, but try to relate it to the prevailing conditions, so that you can get a more accurate estimate of the timing of changes, because this is what you should primarily be interested in.

Timing is everything when it comes to weather. If you know that you have a few hours to go before conditions deteriorate badly, or before the wind changes direction, then you may judge it sensible to press on to your original destination. Alternatively you may think it is time to start looking for shelter until the conditions moderate, and in making these sort of decisions you also need to take into account the strength of your boat and particularly of its crew. In deteriorating conditions it is usually the crew which is the weak point of the boat: whilst the boat itself may be quite able to cope with extended periods of rough seas and strong winds, the crew may be less than able to do so, and this can lead to bad decisions or, worse still, injury. Pressing on to your destination will always be an attractive proposition – completing what you set out to do – and in a well-found motor sailer this should be a possibility provided you can put up with the discomfort which may be involved. However, you have to be aware that judgement tends to become clouded by the lure of the haven ahead, and this is usually the time when things start to go wrong. Another factor to bear in mind is that there is always a risk that the deteriorating conditions could make the entrance to this haven a dangerous proposition.

When running before the wind it is not always easy to appreciate how rapidly conditions are deteriorating as the wind freshens. You don't feel the full effect of the wind due to the forward speed of the boat, and the sea conditions also seem much more moderate when you are running before the wind because you don't see and feel the breaking crests as you look ahead. Neither is there the same dramatic impact on the motion of the boat or the increased noise of the wind in the rigging to warn you. It may not be easy to do under sail, but if you are running under motor it can be a good discipline to turn the boat round every hour or so to get an accurate impression of what the sea conditions are really like. The difference when heading into the sea can be quite frightening.

Another factor to consider when you are running downwind and when your destination is also downwind, is that the same wind which is helping you to your destination could be piling up the seas in the entrance to the harbour for which you are bound; particularly if the harbour has a bar at the entrance and there is an ebb tide running. You could find yourself arriving off a harbour mouth where conditions are less than conducive to making a safe entrance.

All these things have to be borne in mind when considering what course of action to take in deteriorating conditions, and one of the joys of a motor sailer is that very few options become closed to you because of the direction of the wind. With a powerful engine and a hull suited to the purpose, you can make progress into wind even against quite difficult sea conditions, and this can be a very valuable alternative, bearing in mind any sheltered waters will tend to lie upwind rather than down-wind. You may have an uncomfortable time of it in the early stages of heading upwind, but if this is where the shelter lies, the conditions can only get better as you get closer to the land and the shelter you are aiming for.

If you are heading into wind on a motor sailer under power alone, you will want to set the throttle very carefully. Bear in mind that, whilst it is practical to set a throttle speed which will cope with most of the waves which come along, there are always bigger waves lurking in any wave train, and what is a comfortable throttle setting for an average wave could be totally wrong for that bigger-than-average wave that decides to have a breaking crest. It will often be difficult to find a good average throttle setting which is suitable for the conditions, and you should be ready with your hand close to the throttle to cope with any big waves when you see them coming along. You can even drive the boat on the throttle, easing it over the waves matching the speed and the throttle setting to the conditions outside, but this requires a high level of concentration and one which is apt to tire one rapidly.

When driving into a head sea, it is also important not to ease the speed too much. Good steering control is needed in head seas, and this can only be achieved by keeping a reasonable speed on the boat so that the rudder is fully effective. It can often be better and more comfortable to alter course 10 or 20 degrees off the wind: this has the effect of stretching out the wave length to a certain extent, which means that the pitching is less exaggerated and the wave fronts effectively less steep so that the ride is more comfortable. In bad conditions it is even possible to effectively 'tack' the boat upwind under motor, just as you would under sail, in order to make progress to your intended destination whilst getting a more comfortable ride and reducing the stresses on the boat.

The good stability of a motor sailer with a ballast keel does allow safe progress to be made with the seas on the beam even in rough conditions. There is probably less stress operating on the boat in a beam sea than in any other direction, although the motion can tend to be uncomfortable. Once again a small alteration of course may help to reduce the motion a great deal, and certainly in these conditions you must maintain adequate speed in order to keep full steering control. Keep a careful watch out, too, for the odd breaking wave which might catch you unawares and roll down on you. Beam on, a motor sailer is exposing its large superstructure to the waves, and there is no doubt that a heavy breaking wave hitting from this direction could cause structural damage. However, waves rarely break along a long front except in shoal areas; if you do see a breaking wave approaching, it should be possible to head partly up into the wave before it breaks in order to reduce the impact. Alternatively you can steer away from it. By steering away you will, hopefully, buy time to allow the energy of the breaking wave to dissipate, but you are exposing a more vulnerable part of the boat to the breaking wave.

Running before the seas whether under power, or sail, or a combination of both, is not always a sensible way to go if the conditions are deteriorating. A displacement motor sailer has no way of travelling faster than the waves, and so it can be vulnerable to waves approaching from the stern. On other courses a boat can be headed up into the seas, or action can be taken to reduce the impact if a large breaking wave is seen, whereas when running there is very little that can be done except to hold on tight and try and steer a straight course. Keeping the boat directly in front of the wind is quite important because, once a sheer starts because a breaking wave is overtaking the stern, it may be very difficult to control it, and you could end up with a classic broaching position. In any situation where a breaking wave is approaching from the stern, then full engine power is required to give maximum steering effect and also to reduce the impact of a wave. Closing the throttle in this situation can only increase the danger, and you will greatly reduce the steering control just at a time when you want it at its maximum.

Running before a heavy following sea can be an exhilarating experience, but a lot depends on the boat. Motor sailers with pointed cruiser sterns and long, straight keels are probably best equipped for safe progress in these conditions. The stern divides the approaching waves and allows them to pass on each side without either imparting too much additional speed to the boat, or tending to slew it round. The long, straight keel helps to give good directional stability, and a full bow will tend to give plenty of lift to help balance the lift of the stern created by the approaching waves. Broad transom sterns such as can be found on power cruisers are less manageable in these conditions. However, because they tend to give much greater interior space, they are found on motor sailers as well these days.

There may be a temptation to use the motor alone in these rough conditions, because then you have less to worry about. However, the sails can be used to considerable benefit in these conditions, and they can perform three useful functions. They can provide additional headway. They can be used to damp the movement of the hull, and they can be used to improve the steering. Used intelligently, the sails can take a lot of the strain off both boat and crew. Using sails to make additional headway is only likely to happen in a following sea when ideally you want to match the speed of the boat as closely as possible to the speed of the waves. However, when you use the sails it does enable the engine to operate at a lower rpm, thus conserving the fuel supply, which could be crucial if there are extended rough weather conditions. Damping the movement of the hull is probably one of the biggest attractions of using the sails, and the improvement in comfort on board can be very marked. It may allow food to be prepared when this would otherwise have been impossible, navigation can be done with more care and accuracy, and rest and sleep can be taken, all of which make coping with rough conditions much easier. In these conditions the sails are used more for stabilising the steering and reducing the strain on the helmsman than actually carrying out the steering operation itself.

In bad weather the ketch rig has more to offer than a sloop rig because of its greater flexibility in terms of available sail combinations. Apart from the fact that the ketch rig allows the sail area to be reduced without the need to reef, sails can make it easier to handle, and having small sails available at each end of the boat can be used to balance the boat to much greater effect. With a head wind the sails will obviously have no effect on the progress of the boat, but keeping the mizzen sail up and sheeting it in tightly in these conditions could not only help to reduce the rolling, but could have a stabilising effect on the steering. This type of steadying sail is often used to good effect on fishing boats, particularly when it is necessary to keep them head-to-wind during fishing operations; they can offer the same benefits to a motor sailer when hove-to, head to the sea, in bad conditions.

With the wind on the beam, the sails will add to the thrust and increase the speed of the boat, as well as easing the rolling motion. Here you want to keep a comfortable balance, but an alternative could be just to keep up a mizzen sail, which will help the boat point up into the wind rapidly if you see a big breaking wave coming along. In a following wind and sea the sails can be used to enhance the directional stability. A headsail pulling at the bow will tend to keep the bow downwind and lessen the chances of a broach, or help in recovering from a broach if the boat takes a sheer. The shape of a jib tends to provide lift when running before the wind, and this can also be of benefit because it helps to lift the bow up at a time when the seas will want to try and bury it. This lift feature is often used to good effect on catamarans where there may be reduced buoyancy in the bow. By locating the mast further aft, the angle of the jib increases the lift, and thus improves the behaviour of the boat in following seas. Certainly in following seas you should not have the mizzen sail up, and the mainsail will be far less effective than the jib. If you have the mainsail up in these conditions, you also run the risk of gybing.

Having a powerful engine and efficient smaller sails gives the motor sailer owner the means to cope with most situations, particularly in bad weather. In the event of a total engine failure, which is perhaps more likely to occur in rough conditions, then there are still sails available to make progress. Although the ability to make good a desired course may be limited, you should be able to make enough progress to keep out of trouble. The ability of some motor orientated motor sailers to beat off a lee shore may be questionable, but otherwise the motor sailer can be treated as an ordinary sailing cruiser. The poor close-hauling ability on some of the motor orientated types is due partly to the directional stability, and partly by the long keel which can make tacking more difficult, but probably more so by the excessive leeway which the relatively shallow draft allows. This, combined with the relatively small rig and the heavy hull, means that there is inadequate thrust generated to give effective control, although in strong winds, and apart from its tendency to make leeway, there is probably not a lot to choose between the motor sailer and the sailing cruiser.

In really strong winds, above force 8 perhaps, then it tends to become a question of survival rather than making progress. Here different tactics must be adopted, and again the action taken will depend largely on the prevailing conditions and the sea room. With limited sea room to leeward or in the proximity of rocks, shoals or tidal races, then there is very little alternative but to try and make progress to windward. The motor sailer with its strong hull and rig and its powerful engine is as well equipped as most boats to do this.

Heaving-to

Given plenty of sea room, several possible courses are possible: heaving-to, lying a-hull, lying to a sea anchor, or running with warps trailing. Probably the best solution as far as a motor sailer is concerned is to heave-to with the engines turning over at a speed which is adequate to give good steering control and with the wind 40 or so degrees on the bow. Keeping the mizzen up in these conditions would help with steering and enable you to turn head-to-wind very quickly if necessary. Life under these conditions can be pretty uncomfortable, but at least the situation is under control and the strongest part of the boat, the bow, is presented to the sea. Lying a-hull means taking down all sail, stopping the engine, battening everything down securely and letting the boat sort out the problem. Providing you have a strong boat this could be a useful solution, and it certainly reduces the physical, if not the mental stresses on the crew. In this situation the boat tends to give to the waves rather than to fight them which helps to reduce the strains on the hull. The boat will normally adopt an attitude nearly beam-on to the seas, and when a wave strikes will tend to heel and slide to leeward. This could be fine for a smaller motor sailer, but anything over about 40 feet may not give too easily to the wave, because the weight of the boat will make it less resilient, and this could lead to damage and other problems.

Sea anchors and drogues

One hears of sea anchors being put out as the panacea for all the evils of rough seas. This may be fine in theory, but in practice few motor sailers will carry sea anchors, and the chances of rigging one successfully under rough conditions are not good. Some books on rough sea sailing suggest

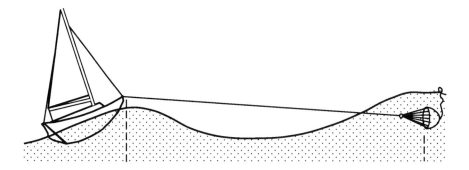

FIG 11 Using a sea anchor from the bow. The scope of the line should be at least one wave length to ensure that the sea anchor stays well in the water and exerts a steady pull.

you can construct a sea anchor from spare materials which may be on board, but I suggest that people advocating this course of action have had very little experience of rough sea conditions. A properly rigged sea anchor can help by keeping the boat head-to-wind in rough seas, allowing the crew to get some rest, but the warps of the sea anchor will need to be tended very carefully and protected from chafe, and the sea anchor itself needs to be well-constructed to take the strain.

The sea anchor is often confused with the drogue, the latter being put out from the stern, and used to stabilise the steering. An option to the drogue can be to trail long warps from the stern, the idea in both cases being to exert a pull at the stern which greatly reduces the stress on the steering and keeps the boat on a steady course downwind, reducing the chances of broaching. With warps or a drogue out at the stern the steering will be much more effective, but if either of these courses of action are to be successful, then you need to be running as fast as

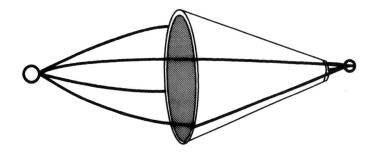

FIG 12 If a drogue is going to be successful it has to be strongly constructed with wire strops and strong canvas. The pull on the line can be up to three tonnes.

possible in order to increase the pull on the stern and the consequent stabilising effect.

It is not easy to make decisions about what to do in rough seas because so much depends on the boat in question, the amount of fuel left, the speed at which conditions are changing, the sea room available and, last but not least, the strength of the crew. Few motor sailer owners have a great deal of experience of rough seas, so that they have to learn as they go along. An owner can do a great deal by thinking about these conditions in advance, and preparing for them mentally and materially in case he is caught out. Maintenance should never be neglected, as analysis shows that a great many of the potential disasters which occur at sea are caused by the failure of components on the boat in the initial stages. Once a failure occurs, your guard is down and you could be starting off the chain reaction that often leads towards disaster. In a motor sailer you probably have one of the best types of craft to cope with adverse conditions, but it will only do the job if it is well-maintained.

CHAPTER 6

ENGINES

The engine on a motor sailer is one of the two alternative propulsion systems. It could be argued that the engine is not particularly critical on a motor sailer because if it doesn't work there are still the sails to fall back on as an alternative means of propulsion. However, as with auxiliary sailing yachts, motor sailers can frequently be put into positions where the reliability of the engine can mean the difference between survival or disaster. Working close inshore or in harbour entrances, for example, an engine failure could be critical to safety, so the engine of a motor sailer should be installed with a view to reliability.

The vast majority of motor sailers use a single engine, which is generally adequate for manoeuvrability and reliability. A twin engine installation would obviously raise the levels of both of these aspects, but against this would be the fact that twin engines occupy more space within the hull and the propellers will offer more drag. In general the engines will also have to be mounted higher in the hull with a twin engine installation, which in turn means a higher deck within the wheelhouse or cockpit. However, if handling under power is a prime requirement, then a twin engine installation is certainly practical and possible, and is an option which is used increasingly on larger motor sailers.

The usual underwater shape of a motor sailer allows a single engine to be mounted low down on the centreline with the propeller shaft coming out of the hull nearly horizontally. At this angle the propeller gives maximum efficiency, and the engine and gearbox lubrication system have the best chance of operating efficiently. Most marine engines are designed to run at angles of up to 15 degrees from the horizontal in the fore and aft direction, and up to 30 degrees in the transverse direction, and the limiting factor here is usually the ability for the oil in the sump to maintain a suitable level for the oil pump to operate satisfactorily. This angle has to take the pitching of the vessel into account, so the steeper the angle of installation, the less the latitude there is to account for when the hull pitches.

In the interests of reducing noise and vibration, most motor sailer engine installations have the engine flexibly mounted on its bearers. The

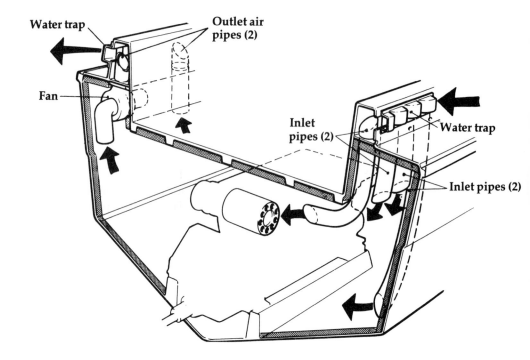

FIG 13 A typical engine compartment ventilation system with one inlet being taken close to the engine air intake and an electric fan at the exit to assist the air circulation. *Drawing by courtesy of Volvo Penta.*

advantages of reducing noise and vibration by this system are gained at the expense of added complication. With the engine on flexible mounts, then all the connections between the engine and the fixed parts of the boat also have to be flexible to allow for the engine movement. This includes the controls, fuel lines, water connections, electrical connections, the exhaust system, and the couplings linking the engine and the gearbox to the propeller shaft. Considerable attention has to be paid to the engineering and installation of these flexible links, which reduce reliability in the sense that they are a potential source of failure. The fact that engines continue to be flexibly mounted demonstrates that the gain in noise and vibration reduction is worthwhile, but all the moving parts necessary to achieve this should get regular inspection in order to identify any deterioration.

For seagoing operations it is important to aim at self-sufficiency. Assistance can be difficult to find when you are out at sea, and it is not always practical to carry a complete set of spares. By careful design it is possible to provide duplication of the essential systems so as to ensure greater reliability; in a broad sense this is already done in the case of a motor sailer by having a combination of sails and engines. As far as is practical, this principle of building in redundancy should be carried over to the engine systems themselves to reduce the chance of being caught out at sea.

Diesel engines

Virtually without exception, every production motor sailer on the market today has a diesel engine; indeed, one of the classifying criterion for a motor sailer could be that it is fitted with a diesel engine. This engine has an inherent reliability not found in petrol engines, largely because it doesn't depend on electricity to keep it running. You may need electricity in order to start a diesel engine, although with some smaller engines this is not always the case and hand starting can be incorporated, but once the engine is running then, whatever happens to the electrical system on board, that engine should keep running. This in itself removes one of the potential causes of failure. However, it should be borne in mind that, with some modern diesel engines, features such as electronic injection and control systems are being introduced by manufacturers in the interests of greater efficiency, and it is unlikely that these electronic diesel engines can be isolated from the requirement for an electrical supply. As far as reliability is concerned, this could be a retrograde step, but then we are already starting to rely on the onboard electrical for such vital items as the radio and position fixing, so extending it to the engine as well is perhaps not such a problem.

Certainly the fact that you have a diesel engine which may run without electrical power once it has been started should not be used as an excuse to cut corners on the electrical installation. This should be installed with a view to providing the same reliability as the diesel engine itself. There is nothing quite like the ability to press the starter button in an emergency and have engine power readily available, and for that facility you need to thank the electrical system as much as the engine itself.

It is very rare these days for the engine itself to fail. You rarely hear of pistons seizing up or valves breaking: modern engines are thoroughly tested and tend to run well within their limits. The risks of failure tend to come from the ancillary systems connected with the engine, such as the electrical, fuel, cooling water and exhaust systems. Often these systems are engineered by the building yard and do not undergo the same rigorous testing as the engine itself. They also suffer more from deterioration, so the owner has a major role to play in maintaining the efficiency of these systems to ensure that they match the reliability of the engine itself.

The general type of diesel engine fitted to motor sailers is a four-cylinder diesel, probably somewhere between 50–100 hp. Modern light-weight diesel engines in this category tend to occupy far less space than some of the single or twin cylinder diesel engines which are a feature of early motor sailer design, again reflecting their fishing vessel origins. These modern multi-cylinder engines also produce less noise and vibration than their earlier counterparts, and have become highly refined power units. In selecting an engine for the task, noise and vibration are important characteristics to consider, particularly when the engine may be in use for long periods of time; this aspect will be looked at in more detail later.

In general, motor sailers tend to be offered with specific engine installations. This is a sound approach, ensuring that the design is more integrated. In some cases, options are available for owner selection: in this situation, one of the main criteria apart from price should be the availability of servicing and spares in the area where the boat will be used. It can make all the difference to operating a motor sailer if a service and spares agent is available in the port where the vessel is based, avoiding the inconvenience of having to send away for spare parts. In the enthusiasm to buy it is easy to forget such aspects of operating a motor sailer, but they can prove vitally important at a later date. If you plan extended cruising with the boat, then the availability of spares and servicing over a much wider area should also be considered.

With modern diesel engines becoming more compact for a given horsepower, there is a noticeable trend towards tucking these engines away in smaller and smaller spaces, an excellent design feature in terms of generating extra accommodation space, but less than ideal when it comes to servicing and maintenance on the engine itself. Easy access to the key parts of the engine is important, particularly to units such as the starter motor which is often installed low down, and the fuel system. Access is obtained in different ways on different motor sailers, but usually involves the removal of top or side panels. These panels can open up directly into the accommodation, making it all too easy to transfer the engine oil and dirt there too: it can be a good idea to have sheets or covers available to protect the carpets and furnishings when tackling engine servicing.

Most engines are designed so that the basic servicing such as checking oil and water levels can be done from the top. Top access is fine as long as the access hatch is protected, but not such a good idea when it opens out into the floor of a cockpit, because this can be a way for water to find its way down below and start corrosion. Top access is certainly feasible if the engine is under the wheelhouse, but it should be possible to open the hatch whilst the boat is underway at sea, either to cope with any emergency, or just for routine checks, without having to disturb everything in the wheelhouse. The top hatch will often be combined with removable panels in the accommodation so that you can get side access to the engine for more extensive servicing.

Engine compartment

The modern trend on motor sailers is to box in the engine in a compartment little bigger than the engine itself in order to expand the space available for accommodation. There is no doubt, however, that the best approach is to have a good sized engine compartment, with an access door which gives you full access to the engine once you are inside the compartment. This is an approach which does demand taking up a fair amount of valuable space inside the boat, but the compensation is that any oil or grease contamination is kept inside the engine compartment, and there is generally space available for installing extra machinery at a later date, perhaps a small generator or even air-conditioning.

In addition to the engine itself the engine compartment also has to house a lot of the auxiliary systems such as water heating, the freshwater pump, the electrical system, and the air-conditioning plant where this is fitted. If an auxiliary generator is installed, then this will almost certainly have to be in the engine compartment as well, so the demands on space can be quite high, and will invariably conflict with the demands for accommodation space. The designer has therefore to walk a tightrope of compromise, which often results in some of these ancillary systems being allocated space in other parts of the boat. Wherever the equipment is located, it should be accessible for maintenance and servicing and it should be possible to take out the equipment without having to cut away sections of the boat.

Ventilation and noise

A diesel engine requires large quantities of air for it to run efficiently. This air serves the dual purpose of providing the combustion air for the engine, and helping to cool the engine compartment. Generally speaking, the combustion air is taken from the general flow of air which enters the engine compartment. In the interests of engine efficiency, this combustion air should be as cool as possible, which is not always the case in a compact engine compartment. One solution is to provide a separate air intake which is ducted directly to the engine itself, but in this case the air intake must have a water trap or some means of preventing spray and water from entering directly into the engine. The air for the engine compartment is usually ducted in through grilles mounted on the side of the wheelhouse or superstructure, but this is not always the most satisfactory location, and fitting them on the inside of the cockpit could give better protection from spray. In addition to introducing air into the engine compartment, an exit for the hot air from the compartment should also be provided so that some form of circulation is maintained. The best arrangement is for the cool, incoming air to be ducted to the bottom of the engine compartment, allowing the hot air to exit through the outlet ducting. This should exit well away from the cockpit or passenger areas. Both the inlet and outlet for the air are positions at which noise from the engine compartment can be concentrated; this should be borne in mind when locating these points, and is an argument against locating them in the cockpit. It is possible to silence them with baffles, particularly the inlet side, and this can be preferable to locating the vents on the outside of the boat.

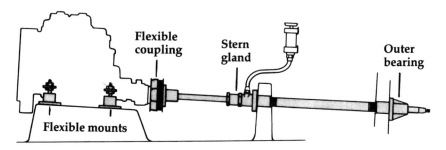

Rubber cushions

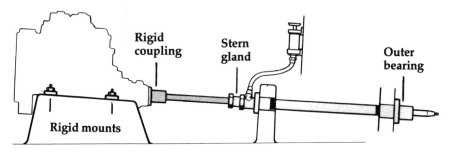

Rigid engine mounting

FIG 14   The difference between rigid and flexibly mounted engines. To allow for the engine movement when flexibly mounted, a flexible coupling has to be introduced into the propeller shaft and all the water, fuel, electrical and exhaust connections to the engine have to have flexible sections. *Drawing by courtesy of Volvo Penta.*

The question of noise is an important one. An incessant high level of noise from an engine compartment can prove very tiring on a long passage. One way to gauge the level of engine noise is to see whether you can hold a normal conversation at the control position when the boat is running at cruising speed. This should be the ideal to aim for, and with modern soundproofing materials it should be feasible to achieve such a sound level. The normal way to deaden engine noise is to line the engine compartment with soundproofing material. This goes a long way to cutting down the noise, but it is equally important to tackle the individual sources of noise: the air inlet and outlet systems, or the propeller itself, where turbulent water hitting the hull can generate considerable noise levels. Normal soundproofing materials are lead based, the lead being a very good absorber of noise; this metal is used in combination with absorbent foams or fibrous material. Whilst it is easy to fit such material around the main panels in an engine compartment, it is difficult to fit it around the transmission areas, but it is only by doing a full soundproofing job that the effects will be properly felt.

One of the major difficulties with soundproofing comes when items such as the electrics or components of the fuel system are mounted on the side panels of the engine compartment. These can make soundproofing difficult, and it is much better if the soundproofing installation is developed during the design of the compartment rather than added as an afterthought. Another good reason for having a walk-in engine compartment is that there is more scope for effective soundproofing, particularly if extra soundproofing is being added retrospectively.

Vibration can also be a major source of noise on motor sailers; this usually applies to the panels and fittings around the engine, which vibrate in harmony. The best way to prevent this is, firstly, to have such panels securely fastened down so that they can't rattle, and then to identify any panels which seem to vibrate in harmony with the engine. These should have stiffening strips or material fitted to reduce the effects of vibration. Much the same approach goes for damping out the propeller noise against the hull; it is usually a question of installing sound damping material on these hull panels and adjacent areas to reduce the harmonic vibration. Trouble taken over soundproofing and vibration elimination will go a long way to increasing the pleasure of using a motor sailer. This is an area where the owner can usually take over and improve things once the boatbuilder has finished his job. Just getting rid of annoying little rattles can greatly increase the pleasure of cruising.

Fuel system

A constant supply of clean, uncontaminated fuel is essential for a diesel engine to operate. The fuel system is probably the greatest area of failure in diesels; by installing a reliable system, the chances of failure are considerably reduced. A lot can be done by making sure, before it gets into the tanks, that the fuel taken on board is clean; this means only refuelling at reliable fuel sources. If there is any doubt about the cleanliness of the fuel from either dirt or water contamination then, where it is practical, the fuel should be passed through a fine filter before it enters the tanks. It is not always possible to be fussy about where a boat is refuelled, and so in spite of these precautions the fuel system on board should be engineered to eliminate the contamination before it gets to the engine.

Where practical, fuel should be carried in two separate tanks with only one in use at any time. This means that if one tank does prove to be contaminated for any reason, there is always a reserve to turn to. If such a system is to be successful, then only one tank should be fuelled from a particular fuel source at a time. The fuel piping should be arranged so that the engine can run off either tank independently, but there should also be a cross feed with valves between the tanks so that the fuel can be transferred to adjust trim, etc, if necessary. In a twin engine installation it should be possible for either engine or both engines to operate from either or both tanks, which does involve more complicated piping and valve systems. Where valves are fitted in the fuel system, then these should be readily accessible, preferably without having to lift the engine

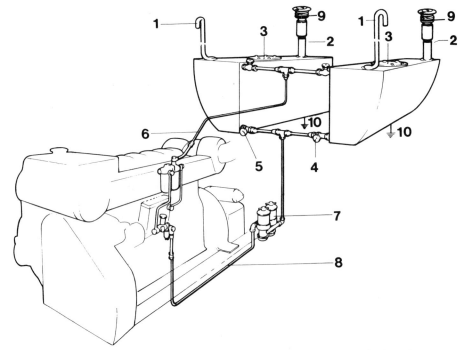

1. Air-venting pipes, min ½″ diameter
2. Filler pipes, steel, min 1½″ internal diameter, joined by means of pipe fitting
3. Inspection covers
4,5 Shut-off cocks, R¾″
6. Return line, external diameter ⅜″ (10 mm)
7. Pre-filter (extra equipment). A vacuum meter must be used when changing the cartridges in the Twin pre-filter while the boat is running. The vacuum meter should be fitted between the filter and the feed pump
8. Suction line, external diameter ⅜″ (10 mm) for max length 20″ (6 m). In the case of greater length, diameter ½″ (12 mm)
9. Deck screw fitting (min 1½″ internal diameter) with rubber fuel-resistant deck sealing sleeve
10. Earth connection

FIG 15 A complete fuel system with two tanks which gives added security if one tank becomes contaminated. *Drawing by courtesy of Volvo Penta.*

room hatches, and the fuel tank shut-off valves should have extended spindles to enable them to be switched off from outside the engine compartment in the event of fire.

Fuel tanks can be either metal or glass fibre. The latter are usually formed as an integral part of the hull and their main disadvantage is that they are difficult to drain and clean. Metal tanks are better in this respect, but they have to be firmly secured against any movement, and ideally both types of tank should be fitted with a manhole to give access to the interior for inspection and cleaning. A tank should be fitted with a sump and a drain valve which allows any water or dirt to be drained off from the bottom of the tank. Draining needs to be a regular operation carried out in calm conditions before the water or dirt level reaches the suction pipe inside the tank. Remember that, at sea, because of the movement of the boat, any water or dirt in the fuel will be churned up and is likely to be distributed throughout the tank. As a precaution against this reaching the engine itself, a fuel filter and water trap are usually built into the piping system before the fuel reaches the engine. Such filters usually have a glass bowl which enables you to see whether there is any contamination, so it can be removed before it gets to danger levels. As a further precaution, the diesel engine itself has a filter with a replaceable element installed before the fuel pump which has to be replaced at regular intervals. Some engines will have twin filters with a switch-over valve allowing a filter to be cleaned or changed whilst the engine is running. With all these precautions you are usually guaranteed that clean fuel will get to the engine itself, provided that you clean or replace filters at regular intervals.

When filling the fuel tanks, the fillers should be out on deck so that any spillage during the operation does not run into the bilges or into the boat. Breather pipes, which should be adequate in size to allow for fast filling, also have to be led out on to the deck to prevent fumes contaminating the accommodation or bilges. Normally the ends of breathers can simply be bent over in the form of a gooseneck when they exit on deck, but now it is common to take them out through the side of the boat. This works reasonably well, although there is a greater risk here of water finding its way through the breather back into the tank. The end of any breather pipe is usually fitted with a fine gauze to prevent water – or at least to reduce the chance of water – entering the pipe, and to reduce the fire risk from explosive fumes coming out of the pipe.

Fuel supply lines from the tank to the engine need to be carefully routed to avoid places where they might get crushed, knocked or chafed. Copper pipes are preferable, but reinforced plastic is acceptable provided it is of a type which has been specified for the purpose. Plastic piping can be more vulnerable in the event of a fire, but both types of fuel piping should be kept well clear of hot exhaust pipes.

With a flexibly mounted engine, part of the fuel line will have to be designed to flex to allow for the engine movement. This flexing should be in reinforced pipe in order to make it as durable as possible. Plastic piping used in this role is liable to harden and crack, and is not entirely suitable in the long term. Most diesel engines also require a return fuel pipe to take the excess fuel not required for combustion back to the tank. This return line needs to be engineered to the same high standards as the main fuel line, simply because any damage or break will pump fuel into the bilges, exhausting your fuel supply rapidly. When designing the fuel system on a twin tank installation, the return pipe must return the fuel into the same tank from which the fuel is being drawn, otherwise there will be an overflow in the other tank and an empty fuel tank on the side being used.

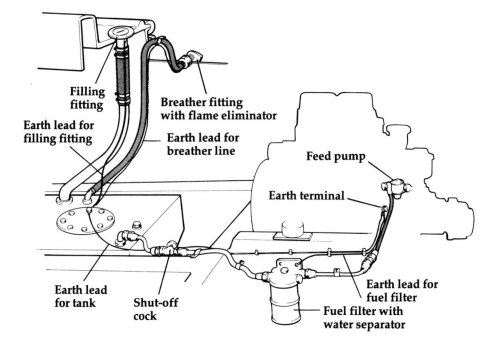

FIG 16 The features of a well engineered fuel system. Note particularly the use of double worm drive clips on the filler pipe, the earthing wire connections between the various components to prevent the build up of static electricity, and the adequate securing of the pipework. *Drawing by courtesy of Volvo Penta.*

Cooling system

The cooling system is designed to carry away waste heat from the engine using fresh and sea water. Practically all diesel engines used on motor sailers today will use fresh water cooling as the primary water cooling; the sea water cooling system then cools the fresh water through a heat exchanger. As the fresh water cooling system is engineered as part of the engine, this can normally be assumed to be reliable, although water pumps can suffer from broken drive belts and thermostats, and hose pipes sometimes need replacing. Otherwise it is generally the sea water system which is more prone to giving trouble, and this needs a particularly high standard of engineering. Water comes into the system through an outlet in the bottom of the boat; this should be protected by an integral seacock, so that the system can be isolated in the event of leakage. A point overlooked on most installations is that, if there is a leakage in the water system, then this valve which is vital for safety will be lost somewhere in the bottom of the bilge, since it will be the first thing to be covered by the incoming water. To be fully effective the spindle of the valve or its operating lever should be extended to above the waterline, or at least outside the engine compartment, so that it can

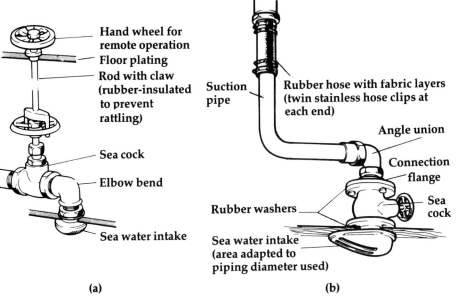

Hand wheel for
remote operation

Floor plating

Rod with claw
(rubber-insulated
to prevent
rattling)

Suction
pipe

Rubber hose with fabric layers
(twin stainless hose clips at
each end)

Angle union

Sea cock

Connection
flange

Elbow bend

Rubber washers

Sea
cock

Sea water intake

Sea water intake
(area adapted to
piping diameter used)

(a)

(b)

FIG 17 (a) A seacock with the valve spindle extended up to deck level. (b) An alternative
water inlet showing the double worm drive clips on the flexible section to give added security.
Drawing by courtesy of Volvo Penta

be operated quickly in the event of an emergency.

From the seacock the water goes into a filter which helps to remove any
solid matter which might cause blockage. This filter can usually be
cleaned with the boat in the water if it does get blocked. One of the first
points of weakness in the system is often at this point, where flexible
rubber hoses take the water up to the heat exchanger. These flexible
hoses can be vulnerable and should be of reinforced material, preferably
rubber rather than plastic. They also need to be secured with double hose
clips. Remember that these hoses are open to the full pressure of the
outside water, and any failure in these pipes or in the sea water cooling
system will allow water into the boat, which will then fill up pretty
rapidly unless prompt action is taken.

After passing through the heat exchangers (there may be a separate
one for the gearbox) and the pump, the cooling water is normally ejected
into the engine exhaust system. The initial part of the exhaust system,
where it leaves the engine, is metal but, as a general rule, large diameter
flexible hoses then take the exhaust gases through to the exit point in the
hull, with perhaps a silencer fitted on the way. These exhaust gases are
hot and, without the cooling water, would melt the rubber pipe. This
means that if there is a failure in the engine sea water cooling system, not
only will the engine get hot, but the exhaust will not have its cooling

water either. This will cause the rubber to melt and could start a fire. The sea water cooling system is therefore obviously vital to the safe operation of the motor sailer. Although it is not a regular fitting, some form of safety indicator which shows if the flow of cooling water has stopped should be considered important. All parts of the engine cooling system should be installed to the highest possible standards using the correct quality hoses and adequate securing clips. Although out of sight is often out of mind, the cooling system is probably the most vulnerable of all the systems on board a motor sailer, and regular checks on the system are vital. This is another good reason for being able to get access to the engine compartment quickly and easily. With the sea water cooling pump normally belt driven from the engine, a useful safeguard is to have a spare drive belt already installed in place but taped up out of the way, so that if the drive belt does break, then fitting a new one is a comparatively simple operation.

Other types of engine cooling systems may be used on motor sailers, but these are generally found on one-off designs. A closed fresh water cooling system using a heat exchanger on the outside of the hull,

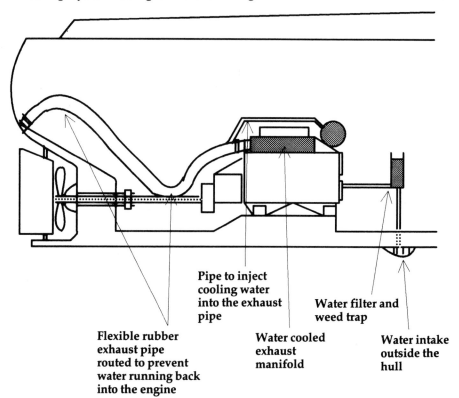

Pipe to inject cooling water into the exhaust pipe

Water filter and weed trap

Flexible rubber exhaust pipe routed to prevent water running back into the engine

Water cooled exhaust manifold

Water intake outside the hull

FIG 18 Important features of the cooling and exhaust systems. Reliability is essential in a sea water cooling system because not only will it allow water into the boat if there is a failure, but the exhaust depends on the sea water injection for cooling. If this water flow stops, then the hot exhaust gases could quickly burn through the rubber exhaust pipe and start a fire.

commonly called a keel cooler, is one option. With such a system you would still need to find some way of cooling the exhaust, and here the best available option is to fit a dry exhaust which is constructed entirely of metal. This has to be very carefully installed because of its high heat characteristics. A similar type of exhaust system would be necessary with an air-cooled engine. Here air rather than water is used for the cooling, with large ducts fitted to get adequate quantities of air in and out of the cooling system; though this is not a particularly practical system on a sea going boat. A keel cooling system is sometimes used for an auxiliary generator.

Exhaust system

Whatever type of exhaust system is fitted, the exhaust gases have to come out into the open air at some point. With a water-injected exhaust, they invariably exit through the hull so that the water that comes out falls straight into the sea. The exhaust exit point needs to be carefully considered because, particularly with motor sailers which have a high wheelhouse towards the stern, the vacuum created by the passage of this wheelhouse through the air tends to suck exhaust fumes back on board, which is extremely unpleasant. Modern exhaust systems tend to exit very close to, or below the waterline, so this reduces the problem of the exhaust being sucked back on board, but for this to be successful, a very high standard of installation and maintenance is again necessary in order to reduce the risk of failure. There are a number of proprietary exhaust fittings on the market which act as silencers or water traps, the latter being used to prevent water running back up the exhaust into the engine when the engine is mounted low down in the hull.

Electrical system

The electrical system on board is now a vital element of motor sailing operation. Not only is it used for engine starting and in some cases operation, but it also provides a vital safety role in terms of navigation equipment, radios, and navigation lights. No longer can electrical systems be considered to be a luxury. They are now vital, and with this in mind they need to be engineered to high standards, and to be designed with a degree of redundancy so that one failure does not destroy the whole system.

The heart of any electrical system on board is the batteries. With a single engine-driven alternator it is now possible to charge two or three batteries at the same time from a single source. This is done by means of a blocking diode, and it enables one battery to be kept just for engine starting, so that after a night at anchor this battery will still be fully charged to operate the starter. The domestic systems will then operate from the one or two batteries remaining, and if they go flat through overuse it is not the end of the world because starting the engine can

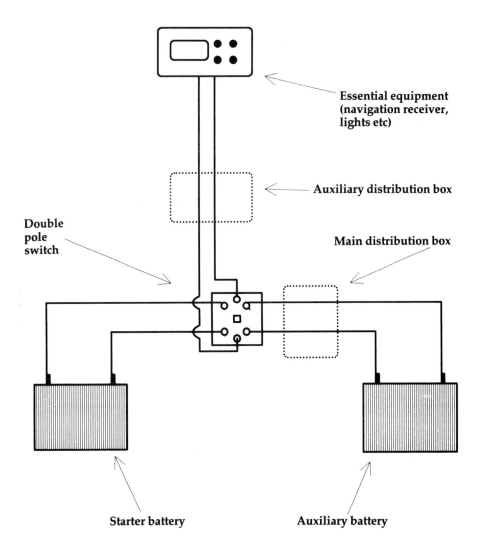

Essential equipment (navigation receiver, lights etc)

Auxiliary distribution box

Double pole switch

Main distribution box

Starter battery

Auxiliary battery

FIG 19 Circuits which would allow essential electrical equipment such as the navigation and compass lights and position fixing equipment to be operated from the starter battery in the event of a failure in the auxiliary battery circuits.

quickly regenerate them. The two-battery domestic system is usually used where a refrigerator is carried on board since this can place high demands on the electrical system. By using a separate battery, the refrigerator supply will not affect the rest of the electrical system.

These days, it can be important to have a separate battery just to operate the electronics. Such a system prevents the surges and voltage variations which can affect sensitive electronics. Another possibility is to have a changeover switch which allows the vital electrical services to be obtained from two alternative battery sources. The diagram shows how this is possible, and it means that there is every chance that essential equipment such as the radio, the position fixing receiver and the navigation lights can be maintained in operational condition even in the event of a major electrical failure.

The double or triple battery installation should guarantee sufficient electrical supplies to meet most requirements, but it is vital to have an ammeter and voltmeter built into the electrical systems so that you can have some check on what is going on all the time. Such meters would give you warning if the alternator stopped working, perhaps through a broken drive belt, but would also indicate whether you are taking more out of the system than the alternator is putting back in, which if allowed to continue will result in flat batteries.

With a modern motor sailer you rely very heavily on the electrical systems to get most of the comforts of home. Items such as refrigerators, water pumps and the lighting can, however, provide a constant drain on the battery when the engine is not being run. After long periods under sail or a night or two at anchor you need to monitor the system quite carefully, looking at the sort of loads that you are taking out in order to manage the electrical supplies.

There are ways of supplementing the charge from the alternator; this can mean using solar panels or air windmill generators. Both will operate just as effectively in harbour or at anchor, and are ways of maintaining the battery charge at no cost after the initial outlay. Both methods of charging are easily connected into the electrical system, but the solar panels will only provide a very small charge which will not compensate for the normal battery drain at sea. However, every little helps, and these systems do provide viable alternatives for those who spend a lot of time under sail. Another option for keeping batteries up to scratch is to have a

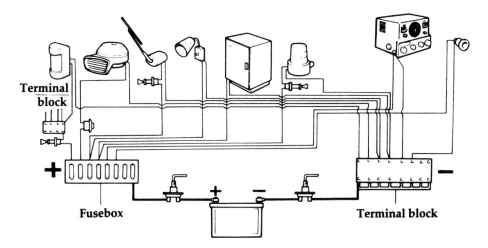

FIG 20   A typical electrical distribution system on a motor sailer.

This wind generator gives an alternative source for electrical power, both in harbour and at sea.

diesel generator able to run independently of the main engine on board. There are noise and cost objections to having an on-board generator, but if you have such items as a freezer, a large refrigerator, or air conditioning on the craft, then a generator is vital in order to maintain them operational at sea. In addition to supplying a high voltage mains supply which allows ordinary domestic electrical equipment to be used on board, the generator can also be used to power a battery charger to supplement the alternator output.

The same type of power supply can be obtained alongside in most marinas by connecting into the shore power supply. This is a favoured option for many motor sailer owners, who are content to use the 12 or 24 volt supply at sea, but are grateful for the high voltage mains supply when alongside the marina which enables them to enjoy all the electrical comforts of home. Where these high voltages are supplied on board, the level of installation must be extremely high, but more importantly they must also be protected from any form of water. Mains voltage electrical equipment should be kept well away from the edges of hatches and doors which might be left open, and the system should be carefully installed with safety devices to reduce the chance of electrical shock. For those with a 12 or 24 volt system, any failure in the system will tend to be an inconvenience. With a 240 volt system any failure could have lethal consequences.

Protecting the on-board electrical system from abuse usually takes the form of fuses or breakers which protect each individual circuit, so that if there is a short circuit or similar problem, the fuse or breaker will isolate that circuit and prevent others being affected. Breakers are better than fuses because they are easily reconnected, but try not to ignore any faults of this nature, and if the problem is a recurring one then search for the cause. Batteries need to be very carefully installed on board to prevent any movement which could damage the large size cables which run from the battery. These heavy duty cables are not protected by fuses, and any failure or short circuit could constitute a fire risk.

Motor sailers can move quite violently on occasions, so the batteries need to be strapped down firmly. Under such conditions, the wiring can also be prone to movement, both through the boat's gyrations and also through vibration, so all the wiring must be adequately secured at closely spaced intervals. Any point where the wiring can rub against sharp edges – when passing through bulkheads, for instance – should be well protected. Any external wiring must be fully waterproof, as must any external fittings such as navigation lights and deck lights. The safety precautions are all common sense, really, but it is still surprising the number of faults and failures that can be found on electrical systems. Probably a large proportion of the faults attributed to modern electronic systems can actually be traced back to the electrical system which supplies them.

Monitoring and servicing

Monitoring systems for the engine and for the other systems on board should be part and parcel of the installation on a good motor sailer. The engine could be running for long periods, so not only should there be gauges to indicate what is happening to pressures and temperatures, but it is also vital to have an alarm system connected to these gauges, since the chance of you actually watching the gauges at the moment something goes wrong is very remote. An audible or visual alarm will immediately alert you to any problem, so that you can either slow or stop the engine and sort it out. There is also no doubt that identifying an engine problem early can prevent very expensive damage at a later date, particularly if the fault lies in the oil pressure or engine temperature systems. Over long periods of running at sea it is important to check the engine oil level at intervals; this normally entails stopping the engine to take a dipstick reading. If you know your engine consumes a certain amount of oil in a certain amount of running, then an automatic topping up system through an installed tank connected by pipe to the engine could be one way of maintaining the lubricating oil level. Such a system could allow you to top up the engine oil simply by opening a valve, which avoids the necessity of trying to juggle with an oil can and funnel on a boat tossing at sea, and also avoids the need actually to stop the engine while the topping up is in progress.

The machinery on a motor sailer is vital to its safety, and indeed it would be safe to say that a reliable engine represents a far better safety measure than all the flares, liferafts and other safety equipment put together. A reliable engine also represents peace of mind and more enjoyable cruising, but this level of reliability will only be achieved through, firstly, a sound and safe initial installation; and secondly, regular maintenance and attention to detail. It sounds obvious, but the machinery is often overlooked until something goes wrong, by which time you could already be in trouble.

The conditions for the machinery on a motor sailer can be very different from those on a motor cruiser. Unlike cruisers, motor sailers can be prone to all the nasty things that happen to sailing boats, such as being knocked down or being swamped by waves. The cockpits can and do fill with water, and the boat can roll heavily, sometimes violently, none of which is conducive to maintaining a reliable engine installation. One of the main principles to observe is that the water should be kept outside under all circumstances, which means having good baffles on the air intakes, adequate protection for the fuel tank breathers and fillers, and protection from drips through hatches or other potential openings into the engine compartment. Everything must be firmly secured – tanks, batteries, ducting, hoses, wiring and generators. If anything moves or starts to come loose it can cause a problem, so prevention here is much better than cure. If you consider what being thrown around, hitting sharp edges, and being doused in spray and water does to your reliability of operation, then imagine what the same conditions are doing to the machinery. Treat the machinery with care, consideration and respect, and you should get the level of reliability which is necessary on a motor sailer.

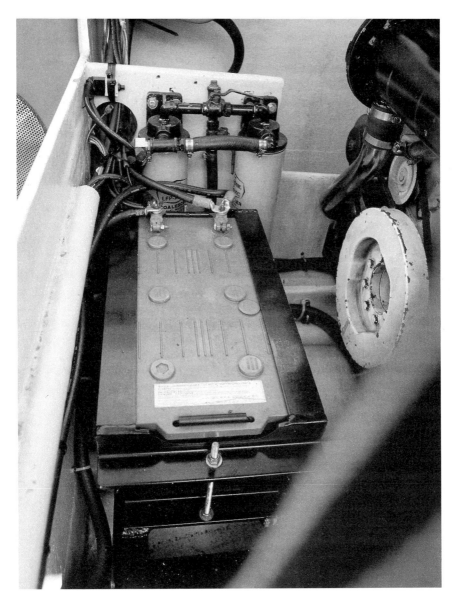

These well engineered battery stowage and fuel systems are the sort of quality needed for reliability. The important items are also readily accessible which helps to ensure the correct standard of maintenance.

CHAPTER 7

━━━━

STERN GEAR

The steering and propulsion systems are some of the most vital parts, yet they are hidden from view and often neglected. Understanding what lies below the waterline and its effect on performance can be very important for getting the best out of a motor sailer. There are a wide variety of options for the stern gear in terms of design and performance; and whilst you can do little about changing them once they are fitted, at least you should understand what is there, how it works, and how to use it to best advantage. The design of both the propulsion system and the rudder will depend to a considerable degree on the type of motor sailer involved, with those orientated towards sailing tending to have a different system from those where the accent is on power. Not only do these underwater parts of the motor sailer have to be designed to get the best out of them in terms of performance, but they are also vital to safety, and so reliability is probably the most important feature of the steering and propulsion. Any failure here can get you into trouble very quickly, and whilst you might be able to cope with the sails as an alternative to the engine, a failure in the steering could render both the sails and the engine ineffective. I would suggest that the rudder and its operating system is the most vital piece of safety equipment on board.

Rudder

Reliability in the rudder is paramount to the safe operation of a boat and can be achieved in two ways. Careful attention to design and construction will give a sound basis, and from then on it comes down to careful maintenance. The maintenance will be minimal, and is really just a question of checking that all is well, and detecting wear before it reaches serious proportions. Every time the boat dries out or is taken out of the water, make certain that this area is checked out. Simply by trying to move the rudder up and down and sideways you will be able to detect whether any wear exists. Any wear will almost certainly be in the lower or heel bearing if one is used, which is subject to considerable strain and abuse, particularly if the boat dries out at a mooring. Sand and grit can get inside this bearing and accentuate the wear.

The top bearing of the rudder also acts as the seal to prevent water getting into the boat, so this gland needs checking at regular intervals to ensure that it is not leaking. It is normal for this top bearing to be grease lubricated, and so a regular application of a grease gun or tightening down on the grease applicator should be part of the routine maintenance. Where no heel bearing is fitted, the lower bearing may be on the rudder stock as in many sailing boat designs, or it may be around halfway down the rudder. In either case it will be the bearing which is most prone to wear, and this will need checking. If you do find play in the bearing, accept that the wear will get progressively worse, so replacement of any worn bearings should be considered at an early stage.

As with many other components of a motor sailer, the rudder has to be designed to operate well in two modes. When operating under sail, the rudder acts solely in the flow of water which runs past the hull to give the steering effect. When motoring, though, the rudder is also operating in the induced flow created by the propeller slip stream, and this can greatly increase the steering effect. The steering effect of the rudder will be proportional to the speed of the boat through the water, and it is also approximately proportional to the size of the rudder. The main difficulty in motor sailer rudder design arises when trying to balance the large size of rudder needed to be effective when sailing in very light winds at slow speed, against the smaller size which will give precise steering when proceeding at higher speeds under motor. Most motor sailers tend to have the rudder on the large size to give effective steering at low speeds. The rudder shape tends to differ from that on pure sailing boats by being wider and shallower. This shape is often dictated by the need to retain a shallow draft and to keep the rudder depth within the overall draft. These are low aspect ratio rudders compared with the deep, narrow, high aspect ratio rudders found on most sailing boats.

Steering system

The designer of a motor sailer has to bear in mind that, not only should the boat turn easily when helm is applied, but the hull should also be able to maintain a steady course when left to its own devices, without undue turning of the wheel. Since directional stability is a requirement directly contradictory to easy turning under the rudder, the designer has to tread a delicate path. The long, straight keel found on many motor orientated sailers certainly helps to give directional stability, but it would certainly need a good sized rudder to turn such a vessel effectively. If you compare this with the sailing boat, which tends to have a high aspect ratio keel to enable it to spin round very quickly, you have two extremes in steering performance. Most motor sailers find a hull shape in between these two which strikes a happy balance. What has to be borne in mind with steering is that it is not just a question of design of the rudder shape and its position; the hull shape too has a considerable effect on the steering. Both the underwater and above water shapes are involved, and where sails are carried these can also affect the steering balance, as we have seen. The effect of the wind on the above water hull shape and surfaces, including sails, is particularly important when sailing, and in Chapter 4 this is considered in much greater depth. It is the underwater shape which is important when proceeding under motor only, but this does also have an influence on the directional stability when sailing.

It is principally the profile, or outline shape of the hull when seen from the side, which affects its turning behaviour. The hull will pivot about its centre of lateral resistance, which is more or less at the geometric centre of the underwater profile. If the main underwater area is close to this point, ie, if the keel is deep at the centre and the forefoot and stern are cut away, then the hull will turn easily and the steering will be light. However, such a boat will not have particularly good directional stability, and the steering will need constant correction to maintain course. If the underwater area is spread out along the length of the boat by means of a long, straight keel, then there will be more resistance to turning, particularly if there is a deep forefoot, because these extreme ends of the boat can exert a considerable resistance to the turning influence of the rudder.

It is these underwater areas at the ends of the boat which largely affect the steering, as they exert a greater leverage around the centre of lateral

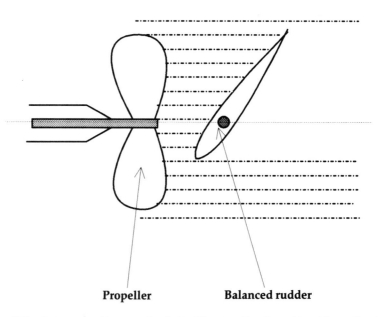

Propeller   **Balanced rudder**

FIG 21   With a balanced rudder operating behind the propeller, the rudder picks up thrust from both sides of the propeller to give a greater steering effect. The balanced rudder has part of the blade forward of its pivot point which reduces the power needed to turn it.

resistance. For maximum effect the rudder should be hung well aft where the turning leverage is most effective, and most modern sailer designs show a cutaway forefoot, which helps the boat to turn easily against the sideways thrust of the rudder. The motor orientated type of motor sailer tends to have a longer, straighter keel which terminates in the rudder, but here the powerful propeller thrust, acting on the rudder when motoring, compensates for any increased difficulty in turning the hull. There are some designs of motor sailer where the rudder is mounted separately from the keel. To a certain extent, this follows sailing boat practice, and it tends to produce a design which turns easily, whilst – provided the keel has been shaped well – also gives reasonable directional stability.

A rudder which is hinged at its forward end will require a considerable effort to turn it, particularly at higher speeds. The rudder also has its own centre of effort, which is the effective point where the turning pressure is exerted. If this centre of effort is some distance from the hinge point, then the leverage on the rudder will be quite high as far as the steering gear is concerned. This can make the steering heavy, particularly when the vessel is proceeding under power at speed. Steering can be a tiring occupation, and a solution has been found with the 'balanced rudder'. This is a rudder where the hinge point is slightly aft of the leading edge of the rudder. This type of rudder has much lower loadings as far as the steering is concerned because, as it is turned, the pressure of water on the section forward of the hinge point wants to turn the rudder; this helps to balance out the pressure on the rear part of the rudder blade, hence its name. The centre of effort of such a rudder will be just aft of the hinge point. The area of the rudder forward of the hinge point should not exceed one fifth of the area of the blade, otherwise the rudder will become very tender, and the steering will tend to lose feel and not self centre. The effect of a balanced rudder will be felt more at high speeds where the pressures on the rudder are greater, which is why balanced rudders are a good solution to the conflicting requirements of providing effective steering at both high and low speeds.

Balanced rudders are particularly effective when mounted behind a propeller. Unlike the unbalanced rudder, hinged at its forward end, which only picks up thrust from one side of the turning propeller, the balanced rudder picks up the thrust from both sides, giving a much stronger steering effect. Balanced rudders are fitted to almost all motor sailers, although styles and shapes vary. Some have the balancing area in front of the hinge only on the lower section of the blade, where it will be less effective in the propeller thrust. Balanced rudders can be particularly effective when manoeuvring in tight quarters, where by putting the rudder hard over and just giving a burst on the throttle, you get a strong sideways thrust with very little ahead movement.

Most rudders are given an airfoil shape in cross section which helps to minimise the resistance of the rudder when passing through the water, but also gives a more effective shape for steering, rather like the lift

A balanced rudder and large propeller aperture on a long keel motor sailer. The balanced rudder will give a much stronger steering effect because it can pick up and redirect the thrust from both the port and starboard sides of the propeller.

generated by an aircraft wing. This lift can generate a slight sideways thrust to windward when the boat carries weather helm and is sailing close-hauled, which can help to compensate for leeway. The airfoil shape also reduces the rudder resistance when sailing in light winds. Another feature found on some rudders is a narrow plate at the top and the bottom of the rudder which, whilst increasing the resistance of the rudder because of the increased wetted surface area, tends to concentrate the water flow across the rudder blade rather than have it creating eddies at the top and bottom.

To connect the rudder to the steering wheel there are several different systems available. One used on motor sailers of the smaller type is the push/pull cable, which is easy to install and effective where the steering loads are not too high. A single cable is generally used, but a more effective installation is obtained by using a double cable so that one cable is always pulling. This double cable installation also gives a measure of redundancy in the event of a failure. The cables require very little maintenance other than a regular check to make sure that there is no wear in the connection fittings.

Probably the most commonly used type of steering on motor sailers is the hydraulic system. This can be an effective system when there are alternative steering positions, with wheels inside in the wheelhouse and outside in the cockpit. Such a system consists basically of a hydraulic pump at the wheel, which is connected by pipes, either rigid or flexible,

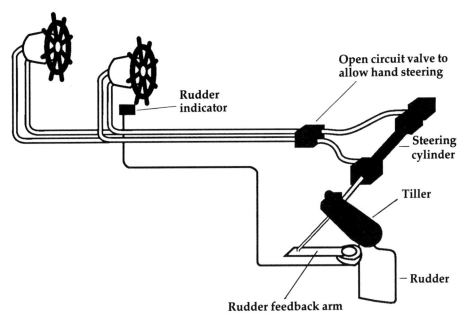

Open circuit valve to
allow hand steering

Rudder
indicator

Steering
cylinder

Tiller

Rudder

Rudder feedback arm

FIG 22   A typical two-station hydraulic steering system for a motor sailer.

to a hydraulic ram which is connected to the rudder via the tiller. A secondary wheel is simply connected into the system using a second hydraulic pump, and either wheel can be used at any time without the other turning and without any changeover. Such a system requires very little maintenance other than occasionally bleeding the hydraulic system for air if the steering starts to feel lumpy or notchy.

Wire and pulley steering is rarely used these days, except in those motor sailers which have a single steering position with an outside wheel, where some of the proprietary systems designed for sailing yachts might be used. Shaft and gear systems are another alternative, and tend to give very smooth steering, but there is a considerable amount of maintenance necessary. The gearboxes require topping up with oil regularly, and checks for corrosion and other problems are needed at regular intervals. There are also more points at which wear can occur.

It is possible to connect autopilots into all these systems, but the most effective types are probably those connected into hydraulic systems, where an electrically powered hydraulic pump provides the steering control. This is a form of power steering, as are most autopilot systems; such a system can be an effective means of control and an alternative to the steering wheel, even when coming in and out of harbour. When considering an autopilot system for a motor sailer, try to get one which has adequate power to move the wheel reasonably rapidly so that this power steering facility can be used to good effect. Power steering as such is rarely found on motor sailers, except in the larger sizes, and is only to be recommended when there are adequate electrical supplies to power the steering system even when proceeding under sail.

Even the best designed and constructed steering systems can fail, and a lot of motor sailers now have an alternative means of steering. This still uses the rudder for the basic steering, but enables the connections to the steering wheel to be bypassed. One of the simplest and most effective is to have the top of the rudder stock accessible either in the locker at the stern, or via an access panel in the deck, so that a tiller can be fitted. The usual system is to have a squared end on the rudder stock, over which a squared socket on the tiller will fit. It may be hard work, but such a system will get you home. To enable such an emergency steering system to operate effectively, the normal steering should be easily disconnectable from the tiller so that it doesn't have to be turned as well. In planning such a system there should be space for the emergency tiller to move over the desired steering angle, and enough space for the helmsman, but both are easily accommodated in the normal stern cockpit.

The gearing of the steering system will depend to a certain extent on the size of wheel which is fitted. The large type of steering wheel found on sailing yachts enables you to exert plenty of leverage, so that you only need one and a half or two turns lock-to-lock for the steering to be effective. Smaller wheels will tend to require more, but no more than three turns should be considered as a maximum. Two to three turns is about right; this gives you a good compromise between the fine steering which you need to maintain the motor sailer on a steady course under sail, and the quick hard-over to hard-over steering which you might need when manoeuvring in harbour. Power steering can reduce the number of turns lock-to-lock, but you do tend to get a loss of feeling with it, which can be a disadvantage when proceeding under sail. It is also something else to go wrong and, quite frankly, should not be a necessary requirement on a well designed steering and rudder system.

Emergency steering

An emergency tiller is one extra worth having, although that will not solve the problem of rudder failure. Should the worst come to the worst and you lose the rudder or it jams, then it should be possible to steer a motor sailer by using the sails alone, balancing the sail area fore and aft by slacking or pulling on the sheets. This could be effective with the wind on the beam, where slacking and hardening in the jib should give reasonable steering effect, but it will probably be much harder to get any useful steering effect from the sail with the wind abaft the beam. You can tow objects astern and pull on ropes on either side to get some sort of steering effect but the key is to try out any emergency systems in moderate conditions before you need them. If a rudder does fail, it is likely to be in a howling gale; having some idea of what to do can help a great deal in such a situation.

Many motor sailers these days are fitted with a bow thruster. These

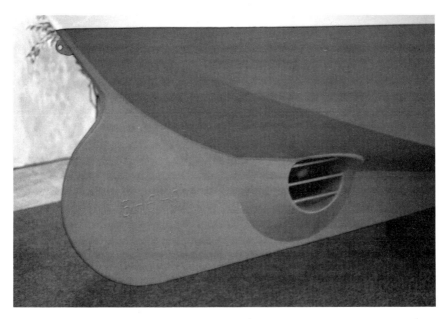

The bulbous bow of a Dutch steel motor sailer. This should help to reduce the pitching motion at sea and help to give an effectively larger waterline length. The transverse bow thruster can help simplify manoeuvring in confined waters.

generally take the form of a propeller fitted in a cross tunnel at the bow. When the propeller is turned, a transverse thrust is generated; reversing the propeller directs the thrust in the opposite direction. An alternative type uses a retractable thruster unit which can be drawn up into the hull when not in use to reduce resistance. Some of these can also be turned in azimuth so the thrust can be directed in any desired direction. This offers the prospect of having a weak but useful alternative means of propulsion as well as a thruster. Even the normal transverse tunnel thruster can provide a viable emergency steering system. Bow thrusters are wonderful for manoeuvring in harbour and can be particularly valuable when operating short handed. They can make the handling much more precise and this, combined with their potential emergency role, makes them a valuable fitting. The smaller sizes are usually electrically powered, whilst hydraulic power is used for larger versions and for the azimuthing types.

Propulsion systems

There are three main types of propulsion system commonly fitted to motor sailers. One is a conventional drive system which runs through a gearbox and then to a straight propeller shaft. This emerges from the hull, usually at a slight downward angle. A similar system uses a controllable pitch propeller, so that in theory a gearbox is not required.

The third is the sail drive system, where the drive is taken through two right-angles and a vertical shaft to produce a compact drive unit.

The conventional system is probably the one most widely used because it is tried, tested and reliable. The gearbox will normally have a reduction of 2:1 or 3:1, cutting down the engine speed to a slower propeller speed. Where the shaft passes through the hull, a gland is fitted. This can be water, oil or grease lubricated, the latter being the most common. This gland will need occasional adjustment to keep it tight, and needs to be felt occasionally when the boat is on a long passage to make sure it is not too tight and running hot. Whilst grease or oil is used to lubricate the front bearing on the stern tube, the aft bearing is commonly water lubricated, the water being picked up by small ducts extending into the water flow which force the water through the bearing.

The controllable pitch propeller may have a clutch instead of a gearbox between the engine and the propeller shaft, although a reduction gearbox would normally be fitted to reduce the engine speed; the clutch

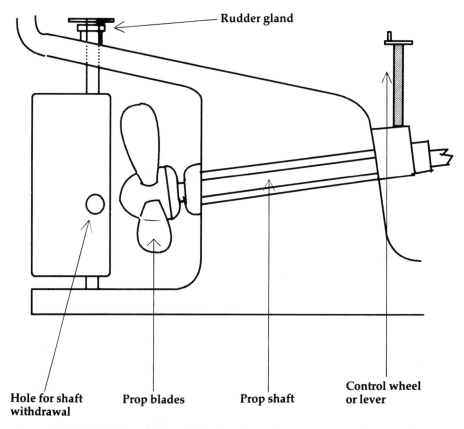

Rudder gland

Hole for shaft withdrawal   **Prop blades**   **Prop shaft**   **Control wheel or lever**

FIG 23 A controllable pitch propeller, which allows the engine to run at a constant speed whilst boat speed is varied using the blade angle. The control wheel or lever would generally be in the cockpit. The hole in the rudder is a feature found on many motor sailers, allowing the propeller shaft to be withdrawn without removing the rudder.

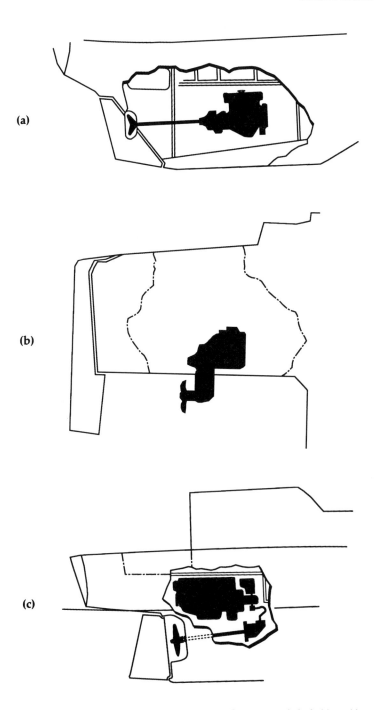

FIG 24   Alternative motor sailer engine installations. (a) Conventional shaft drive with horizontal or near horizontal shaft. (b) A sail drive unit where engine and propulsion are closely integrated. (c) A hydraulic drive system where an engine driven hydraulic pump powers a shaft connected hydraulic motor. This is a similar layout to a mechanical vee-drive installation which allows the engine to be mounted further aft.

can be fitted inside this gearbox. The clutch is quite important because, even though the controllable pitch propeller has a neutral of sorts, the clutch enables the engine to be run independently of the propeller. This can be useful when checking the engine for faults or when running the engine for battery charging in emergencies. The controllable pitch propeller has blades whose angle can be changed either through hydraulic or mechanical systems running down through the centre of the propeller shaft. This increases the mechanical complexity of the system, but modern systems are very reliable, and the controllable pitch propeller is really an infinitely variable gear system which enables the propeller to be matched to the load. By varying the blade angle, reverse can also be selected, and because creep speeds are also available, such a system can make manoeuvring in harbour a more precise operation. Controllable pitch propellers are more expensive compared with conventional systems and, in the event of propeller damage, will certainly be more expensive to repair. This probably explains why they are not a common fitting on motor sailers, although the benefits can be quite notable, particularly where these propellers can be feathered to reduce the resistance when under sail.

It is possible to get propellers which feather automatically when the propeller shaft is not turning, but these are generally only suitable for powers up to around 20 hp, and are therefore unsuitable for motor sailer applications. Most of these automatic feathering propellers have the blades folding in a fore and aft direction to minimise the resistance when not in use, and because of this they tend to be two-bladed propellers which do not have good enough thrust characteristics for motor sailer use. However, a notable exception is the Autoprop, which is not only an automatic feathering propeller, but it is available to handle power outputs. This will match the requirements of most motor sailers. It is available in three-bladed versions and, like other feathering propellers, the Autoprop simply bolts on to the propeller shaft, with no other connections required. The specially shaped blades adopt the feather position when there is no load on the propeller, but as soon as the engine starts to drive the propeller, the blades move into a propulsion position and give effective thrust. Although not generally specified as a standard fitting, the Autoprop could be a worthwhile alternative to motor sailer owners who are looking for effective performance under sail and want to reduce drag.

The sail drive system of propulsion certainly has advantages from the boat builders' point of view. Here the engine and the drive form one integral unit which is simply mounted in the hull. Because it is designed and built as one unit, and has been thoroughly tested, it should have improved reliability. The sensitive point of any such installation is going to be the seal which connects the drive unit to the hull because, although the engine and the drive are solidly mounted together, the whole unit is flexibly mounted, so that a flexible seal has to be installed to allow for the movement. Most manufacturers of this type of system fit a double seal to

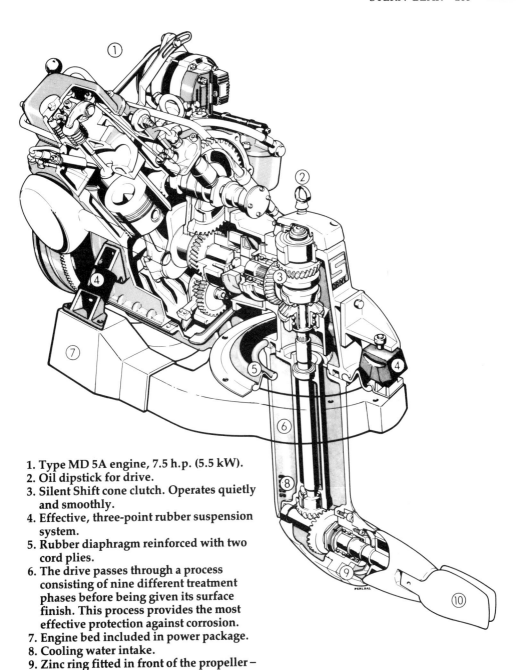

1. **Type MD 5A engine, 7.5 h.p. (5.5 kW).**
2. **Oil dipstick for drive.**
3. **Silent Shift cone clutch. Operates quietly and smoothly.**
4. **Effective, three-point rubber suspension system.**
5. **Rubber diaphragm reinforced with two cord plies.**
6. **The drive passes through a process consisting of nine different treatment phases before being given its surface finish. This process provides the most effective protection against corrosion.**
7. **Engine bed included in power package.**
8. **Cooling water intake.**
9. **Zinc ring fitted in front of the propeller – effective protection against corrosion. Easy to replace when necessary.**
10. **Folding propeller. Several propellers, both conventional and folding, are available for the S-drive.**

FIG 25   The mechanics of the Volvo Penta sail drive installation.

give added security, but this seal should certainly be included as part of the routine checking of the system of the boat because any failure here is going to let water in, in no uncertain manner. The seals on some units are fitted with a water detection device to give warning of any leaks. With these sail drives the final drive shaft to propeller is horizontal; this will give more efficient propulsion compared with the angled propeller shaft found on most other systems. There is generally the option of a two-bladed feathering propeller or a three-bladed fixed one.

Propellers

The propeller itself is an area where there has to be compromise in motor sailer design. When under power the propeller is required to transmit all the engine power into forward thrust. When sailing, a propeller becomes an appendage, producing drag and hindering the progress of the boat; the larger the propeller and the greater the number of blades, the greater the drag. Propulsion is probably one of the areas where the compromise between the motoring and sailing requirements can provide the greatest difficulties for the designer, and the solution will depend a great deal on whether the vessel is to be motor or sailing orientated. In the motor orientated motor sailer there will be little compromise regarding the design and installation of the propeller, and its drag under sail will be

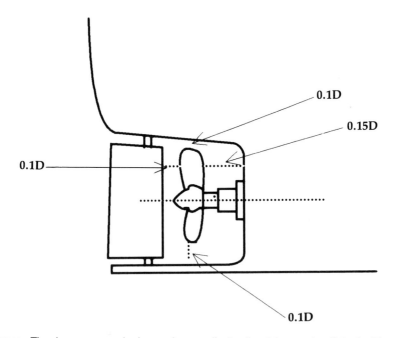

FIG 26   The clearances required around a propeller to allow it to operate efficiently. The clearance between the propeller and the stern tube bearing should be approximately half the propeller shaft diameter. The clearance between the propeller and the rudder should also allow for propeller removal without the need to remove the rudder.

acceptable. The design of the propeller will then only be limited by the space in which it has to turn and the power available.

The space available for the propeller is important for efficiency, but can be limited because, to enable the boat to take the bottom comfortably, the propeller does not normally project below the bottom of the keel. However, for maximum efficiency, the propeller needs to be as large as possible, the larger, slow-turning propeller being the most efficient. In most motor orientated motor sailer designs there is usually adequate space to fit a large propeller, yet still to retain the protective support of the keel extension under the propeller which is used to support the rudder. If a propeller is to work efficiently, then it is also important that there is adequate clearance between the tips of the blades and the surrounding hull. The minimum clearance acceptable should be one sixth the diameter of the propeller. Where the propeller is working behind a deadwood, as is almost invariably the case on a single-engined motor sailer, there should also be a clearance of a similar amount between the deadwood and the leading edge of the propeller blades. These clearances give the propeller a chance to work in reasonably undisturbed water, although the flow of water around the deadwood will always create a degree of disturbance in the propeller flow.

The pitch of a propeller determines the amount that it will move forward with each revolution. Related to the propeller rpm, the pitch will give an indication of the speed; it is from these figures that the designer comes up with the optimum pitch and diameter of a propeller for a particular application. These calculations are complicated by the 'slip', which is the difference between the theoretical advance of the propeller for one revolution and that obtained in practice. This slip is a measure of the efficiency of the propeller design; a good design will produce a slip in the region of 10%. There is also a relationship between the pitch and the diameter for the best efficiency. The pitch/diameter ratio is the critical figure here; for motor sailers it should be between 1 and 1.5. This gives what is termed a 'nearly square' propeller, where the pitch and the diameter are equal or nearly so. Further complications arise with the selection of the number of blades for the propeller, and its shape. Propeller design is a complex subject, and one where there is little substitute for experience. A well designed propeller can make quite a difference to performance, and on production motor sailers a lot of effort is put into optimising the propeller design.

On most motor orientated motor sailers a three-bladed propeller is chosen to give the best compromise. Sailing orientated motor sailers may use two-bladed propellers. Whilst these can now be designed to give useful thrust characteristics, they do tend to increase vibration levels, because when the propeller is mounted behind the deadwood, both blades are blanked off by the deadwood at the same time, whereas with a three-bladed propeller this blanketing of the propeller blades is done on a gradual basis which keeps vibration down. Careful fairing of the deadwood can help to reduce vibration. One advantage of the two-bladed propeller is that it can be 'parked' behind the deadwood when sailing to help reduce drag. However, on balance the three-bladed propeller would be the choice for most types of motor sailer, and provides the most effective compromise. The effect of propeller drag is often over-estimated, and it is rare on motor sailers that one is trying to get the last ounce of speed and performance out of the boat, so that the reduction in speed generated by propeller drag is generally acceptable. It will be most noticeable in light wind sailing.

There is often discussion about whether a propeller creates more drag when it is trailing, ie free to turn when not under power, or when it is locked in position. There is little doubt that with a two-bladed propeller locked out of the way behind the deadwood there is reduced drag. With the three-bladed propeller there will be less drag when the propeller shaft is locked, because when the propeller is free to turn, the friction of the shafting and the reduction gearing will add to the overall resistance. In addition, a propeller left free to turn when the boat is sailing can cause increased wear. Some gearboxes are lubricated with an oil pump which is driven by the input shaft, so if the propeller is trailing, lubrication of the gearbox is inadequate.

To lock the propeller shaft, one of the normal systems is simply to engage the gearbox in ahead or astern gear, which provides an effective lock. Alternatively there are other devices, ranging from simple clamps to sophisticated automatic devices but, as with most things at sea, simplicity is the essence, and if any clamp or lock is fitted then there should be an indication at the steering position that the shaft is locked so that you don't start the engine and try to run it with the lock in place. With a two-bladed propeller, which needs to be locked behind the deadwood, then some mark on the propeller shaft or engagement on the locking system should ensure that the propeller is in the right position.

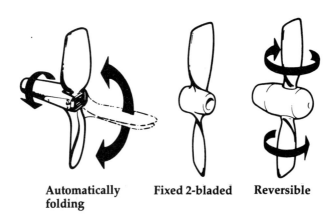

Automatically folding   **Fixed 2-bladed**   **Reversible**

FIG 27   Alternative types of two-bladed propeller which can be found on motor sailers.

Maintenance and damage

There is little maintenance to do on the propulsion system other than simple checking and greasing the stern gland. Where a water lubricated shaft bearing is used, the little scoops which direct water into the bearing have a habit of getting blocked by barnacles and other debris, so each time the boat is out of the water, one of the routine jobs should be to clear these scoops and make sure that a free flow of water can be maintained into the bearings. Without the flow of water, these water lubricated bearings will tend to wear very rapidly. Another of the routine checks should be to try and lift the shaft vertically to check whether there is any movement or play in the bearing indicating wear.

Ropes and plastic can play havoc with propellers. Whilst – on a well regulated boat – there shouldn't be any possibility of ropes from the boat getting into the water, in today's debris-strewn waters, plastic sheets or floating ropes often cause problems. Propeller fouling in this way will quickly become evident from the sluggish performance; with a bit of luck you may be able to get the propeller free simply by putting it into reverse. However, a more serious problem can occur if ropes or plastic finds its way into the gap between the propeller and the shaft bearing housing. Here friction between the two will tend to melt synthetic rope or plastic, making it extremely difficult to clear without dismantling. Because of this danger, the gap between the propeller boss and the bearing house is made as small as possible, and is generally covered by a rope guard, but a good fitting to consider is one of the patented designs of rope cutters which are now available: these will cut through any rope which may find its way into the vicinity of the propeller. Whilst these work well with ropes, they are less effective with plastic sheeting.

In systems where the engine and gearbox are flexibly mounted, there has to be some type of flexible coupling between the gearbox and the propeller shaft to allow for this movement. The propeller shaft is rigid so any flexible coupling has to rely on movement in all directions. These flexible couplings usually incorporate some form of shock absorber, so if the propeller does strike any object under water, there is a certain degree of cushioning built in which hopefully will prevent damage to the propulsion system.

Propellers are usually made from bronze, but sometimes from stainless steel. Either of these metals could react with steel fittings on the hull through electrolytic action which can lead to corrosion. Corrosion tends to be generated by the use of dissimilar metals in the stern gear or in skin fittings, and here you may find the rudder made from mild steel, the propeller from manganese bronze and the propeller shaft from stainless steel. When combined with seawater, you have all the ingredients for electrolytic corrosion; the remedy is to fit zinc anodes to the hull in the vicinity of the stern gear. It is these zinc anodes, rather than the metal fittings of the boat, which take the corrosion, so no harm is done. These zinc anodes are often fitted to the rudder itself as well, and will need replacing as they become eroded, probably on an annual basis.

Motor sailer designers today are recognising the vital role which the stern gear plays in motor sailer design, both in terms of improving the handling characteristics and in terms of safety and security. For the motor sailer owner, understanding what is going on under the water is important in order to get the best out of the craft. Because of the vital role of these fittings, it is important to check them at every opportunity. Don't take chances in this area: if you find problems, do something about them immediately, because they will certainly not get better with time. The last thing you want is a failure in this area at sea, because there will be very little you can do about it then. Very little maintenance is needed on the stern gear, but what is needed is vital, and time spent on maintenance will be time well spent.

CHAPTER 8

DECK AND SUPERSTRUCTURE

The deck and superstructure play a vital role in the design of any motor sailer. They have to be designed to cope with a variety of functions. Practical considerations, such as providing space for working the sails, and a position from which to control the boat, have to be balanced against the appearance of the craft, on which the deck and superstructure obviously have a big impact. All these different functions interact, and in many cases they can conflict, particularly on smaller motor sailers where there can be a limited amount of space available to accommodate all the different requirements.

Appearance

It is very easy to think that practical considerations should outweigh appearance. Motor sailers are essentially practical craft designed for practical yachtsmen, but even practical yachtsmen want a boat to look pleasing. Incorporating an enclosed wheelhouse or steering shelter whilst still retaining an attractive appearance can call for all the skills of a yacht designer, who needs to come up with a final compromise which is both harmonious and practical. From a commercial point of view, it is important that the boat's appearance presents a positive and satisfying first impression. The superstructure of a motor sailer is its most distinctive feature, and the one which tends to set it apart visually from other yachts.

Sheer line

One of the major elements in terms of the appearance will be the sheer or deck line. The most common sheer line is the traditional one of a concave curve, rising at the bow and stern and dipping amidships. This line reflects that of traditional fishing vessels where the high ends at the bow and stern offered protection from the waves, whilst the low waist amidships provided a good protected working area for handling fishing nets. Such a sheer line is commonly used on motor sailers in a fairly pronounced form, reinforcing the traditional appearance of the craft and its emphasis on seaworthiness. Although such a traditional concept meets all the appearance requirements for motor sailer fans, it does have the negative effect of reducing the available headroom inside the hull amidships, just at the point where it is most in demand.

With this type of traditional deck line, the headroom can be increased by using a coachroof over the accommodation. On smaller motor sailers below 40 feet in length, a coachroof is an almost mandatory feature, where the increased space and headroom which it generates are more at a premium. Whilst with traditional wooden construction, using a coachroof introduces a weakness into the deck structure because of the changes in continuity of the deck beams, with modern GRP construction it is a comparatively simple matter to maintain strength in the deck and superstructure moulding, so that the coachroof can easily be accommodated. The coachroof does serve the practical purpose of providing a fastening point for handrails, which make it easier and safer to move about the deck in rough conditions, and the sides of the coachroof also provide a place where windows can be installed to give light and air down below, thus reducing the need to cut holes for windows in the sides of the hull. On larger motor sailers, a flush deck may be used where there is adequate headroom below, and this can give the craft a low, sleek profile, which can be equally attractive.

There is a trend in many modern motor sailer designs to introduce a straight sheer line, or even a reverse sheer. The result is a dramatic increase in the amount of space below, but from an aesthetic point of view it is not always easy to reconcile this type of sheer line with the traditional motor sailer appearance. Using a concave sheer line allows the coachroof and the wheelhouse to sit comfortably tucked down on the hull, which helps to keep the various elements of the structure in proportion. With a straight or reverse sheer, however, the wheelhouse tends to sit on top of the boat in rather stark profile, giving the designer the difficult task of trying to make it look like an integral and attractive part of the design. Straight or reverse sheer lines also produce high top sides amidships, which can make the recovery of objects or survivors from the water a difficult task, thus emphasising the practical advantages of a traditional concave sheer line.

Wheelhouse

Matching the sheer line with the wheelhouse design is one of the more difficult aspects of motor sailer design. When a fully enclosed wheelhouse is used, particularly in the larger sizes, this can be a very dominant feature of the design, particularly on motor orientated motor sailers. The wheelhouse has to be carefully sited if it is to be in harmony with the rest of the boat; in order to balance the bulk of the wheelhouse a concave deck sheer is often exaggerated, so that the high bow provides a visual foil for the large wheelhouse. The natural location for the wheelhouse is over the engine compartment, because the raised deck of the wheelhouse creates a space underneath which is the sensible location for the machinery. However, if the wheelhouse is to have full headroom, its top will be quite high above the deck. This height is also necessary in order to give clear visibility from the wheelhouse when there is a pronounced sheer line with its corresponding high bow.

Conflicting with the ideal of a large, fully enclosed wheelhouse with ample headroom is the requirement of the sail rig where, for maximum efficiency, the boom should be as low as possible (see photo on page 6 Chapter 1). The boom obviously has to swing clear of the top of the wheelhouse, but the sail area needs to be kept low in order to reduce the effect of the wind pressure on the sails and its consequent effect on stability. Motor sailer designers have come up with some interesting solutions to these conflicting problems.

There are a tremendous variety of options open, not only in terms of the location of the wheelhouse, but also the type of wheelhouse, and/or open cockpits which give an alternative steering position. The fully enclosed wheelhouse is a popular option found on a large number of motor sailer designs, particularly those required to operate in colder countries where the fully enclosed arrangement creates a comfortable environment for the crew whatever the conditions outside. One option with such an arrangement is to have full height and full width doors which open out into a cockpit, on or nearly on the same level as the wheelhouse floor, so that the wheelhouse can be opened out in fine weather. This arrangement makes it easy to move around from inside to outside the boat, but it does introduce problems with the drainage of any water which comes on board into the cockpit, and some form of step is necessary to prevent this water getting into the wheelhouse. The large doors would need to be reasonably watertight should any solid water come into the cockpit in rough conditions.

On some motor orientated motor sailers the enclosed wheelhouse provides the only steering position on board, but there is a trend towards having dual steering positions, one inside and one outside, which gives more flexibility in the way in which the boat can be operated depending on the prevailing weather conditions. Such an arrangement does add complication, and on smaller motor sailers can put a lot of pressure on some of the premium areas on the boat, with the additional steering and control systems taking up valuable space. Twin steering positions tend to be a feature of motor sailers over the 30 foot mark, but you have to bear in mind that each steering position detracts from the space available for leisure.

The location of the wheelhouse is another factor which has to be borne in mind in connection with the general layout of the vessel. With an increasing trend towards having the accommodation laid out with an aft cabin which offers privacy to the owner, the wheelhouse has moved from its traditional aft location to one more amidships on many modern motor sailer designs. In this location the wheelhouse becomes rather like the centre cockpit found on some sailing yachts, but with a lid over the top,

This wheel shelter offers protection at both steering positions; it also protects the electronics. There is a good seat in the wheelhouse, but outside it is standing steering only.

and this provides a versatile arrangement, particularly where a secondary steering cockpit can be incorporated aft. Such an arrangement does not work too well with the traditional box-like wheelhouse, so the amidship type of wheelhouses tend to be lower in profile, literally just the height of the windows above the deck, and matched to higher topsides and a straight sheer to maintain the internal space requirements. The steering may be inside this low wheelhouse, or this area may simply be a deck saloon which terminates at its aft end in a steering shelter. Such an arrangement would have sloping front windows; the stepped appearance of the superstructure helps to give the boat a sleek appearance. With the low type of sunken wheelhouse there can be problems with visibility from the forward windows because these are virtually at deck level.

Although the deck structure is called a wheelhouse since its primary function is for steering and controlling the boat, its location above decks and in one of the most comfortable areas of the boat also ensures that it becomes a major social area on board. It is important that its size matches this function. The small wheelhouse with room for a couple of seats will not be adequate to house the average crew on a motor sailer: when the boat is on passage, the majority of the crew will want to be up in the wheelhouse enjoying the sights and free from the sometimes seasickness-inducing environment down below. Although, as we have seen, motor sailers are often descended from fishing boat concepts, the

Social and operational areas mix in the wheelhouse of this motor sailer. Whilst the helmsman has an adequate forward facing seat, the rest of the crew have to make do with the side settees which give a poor outside view and nothing to hold on to when at sea.

type of small, narrow wheelhouse found on fishing boats is not suited to motor sailer use. Any wheelhouse provided should be capable of seating comfortably the whole of the crew when at sea; it will also provide a valuable social area when in harbour.

Whilst the fully enclosed wheelhouse is favoured by many because of the secure weather protection it offers, there is a breed of motor sailer which uses a steering shelter rather than a fully enclosed wheelhouse. The steering shelter offers a degree of protection, but because it tends to be open at the rear, it cannot be heated. The protection offered is therefore mainly from wind and spray rather than from cold and damp. These steering shelters tend to be of lighter construction than the fully enclosed wheelhouse, and certainly look lighter in appearance. In most cases they can be made fully enclosed by canvas screens which zip or clip into place to provide a comfortable enclosure, although such screens are rarely fully windproof and certainly cannot offer the same sort of luxury and weather protection as the fully enclosed wheelhouse. However, they do provide a compromise between the conflicting requirements of operating a motor sailer in warm and cold conditions, and they tend to obviate the need for a secondary cockpit, because the steering shelter will encompass the main control area as well as the outside seating area normally provided by a separate cockpit. Most steering shelters can be found partly enclosing centre cockpits, or located further towards the stern where they partially enclose a more conventional cockpit arrangement. Because they meet the requirements of both closed and open steering positions, only one steering position is normally necessary, but when fitting electronics the sometimes illusory protection offered by the steering shelter will not necessarily offer the full protection required for the water sensitive electronic equipment. With a steering shelter the access door leading down into the accommodation also needs to be fully watertight, because with the open rear of the shelter, this door provides the main defence against water ingress into the hull in rough conditions.

A further option which is found on a few motor sailers is the collapsible shelter. This is usually incorporated around a fixed windscreen, rather like the flybridge steering position on a powerboat. In fine weather this gives a good open steering position, and for bad conditions the cockpit can be enclosed with canvas screens and shelters. These give a degree of protection, but can produce irritating drips and drafts unless they are very carefully constructed and maintained. Canvas screens can look viable and practical when seen in the brochure, but after a bit of wear and tear can start to let in the weather, and it is arguable whether it is better to have no protection at all rather than this rather illusory form of protection.

Aft cabin and cockpits

Whilst an aft cabin is a very nice feature to have in terms of the privacy it provides, it may also demand the installation of a traditional coachroof aft of the wheelhouse or cockpit. On smaller motor sailers this tends to complicate the deck layout arrangements and leave less space to the requirements of working the boat. The centre cockpit and aft cabin layout is often used in conjunction with a ketch rig, which in turn means additional rigging and ropes in the stern of the vessel. This can become a very congested area, making it difficult to move around the boat comfortably, and restricting the amount of space available for the crew in good conditions when lounging up on deck is an attractive pastime. Another point to consider with an aft cabin is access. It is fine with an enclosed wheelhouse, where dry access to the aft cabin is easily available, but when the access to the aft cabin is a forward facing door into an open cockpit, then it can be an unpleasant experience coming out into the wind and spray. On a small motor sailer, trying to squeeze an aft cabin into the accommodation can be rather like trying to squeeze a quart into a pint pot; whilst it may look practical at first glance, aft cabin arrangements are something that you really want to try out at sea before committing yourself.

Without an aft cabin, the wheelhouse can open into a good sized cockpit in the stern of the boat, with the rear bulkhead of the wheelhouse forming the mounting panel for an outside steering position and engine control station. Cockpit lockers fitted in this area can give plenty of stowage for ropes, fenders and all the other bits and pieces of deck gear which are required on most motor sailers and which all seem indispensable. On a motor sailer with an aft cabin, it may often be difficult to allocate adequate space for this type of stowage. Stowage is a major problem on most sailing craft, and you need to be particularly aware of this when you see the plans of a motor sailer. What at first glance may seem an entirely practical arrangement with every spare inch utilised, will allow no room for the extra bits and pieces that seem to collect on board.

Decks

In the search for extra accommodation space, there is a tendency to restrict the working area on deck. This really is a false economy, as much of the pleasure of having a motor sailer comes from having space to move about easily on deck, and the general size of motor sailers is large enough for this to be expected. Safety also comes into it, for if one has to go on deck in bad weather to handle sails, then the ability to move around quickly and easily can be very important. The wheelhouse, particularly if it is the full width of the coachroof, can create narrow side decks which will restrict easy movement on to the foredeck from the cockpit. If the wheelhouse has vertical sides, then getting past it on the narrow side decks might mean leaning out over the side of the boat. Good handholds in the right place are partly the answer, but it helps a great deal if the sides of the wheelhouse are sloped inwards and the side decks wide enough to allow easy passage. Because boats spend such a large proportion of their time in harbour, and owners tend to be looking as much for comfortable accommodation as for practical seagoing ability, more and more designers are placing a stronger emphasis on the internal arrangements, often at the expense of the external layout. Motor sailers should be designed for practical cruising, and so the deck layout should not be compromised too severely.

On larger motor sailers, deck space is not usually a problem. A low or non-existent coachroof can produce large, uncluttered deck areas which from a practical point of view make sail handling much easier, and can also be used for sunbathing. However, simply because they are uncluttered, moving about these open decks in a seaway can be difficult unless lifelines are fitted. On a smaller boat, handholds can be fitted along the top of the coachroof, which can make movement relatively easy and safe; the same sort of handhold arrangements need to be extended past the wheelhouse to allow safe transit in this area.

Guard rails and bulwarks

It could be argued that the guard rails or lifelines which are fitted around the edge of the deck are there to hold on to when moving around the deck, but in general they are very difficult to grip securely because they are narrow, cross-section wires, and difficult to brace against because they flex. The prime purpose of these guard rails is to offer protection should you slip or roll towards the side of the boat; they should stop you from falling overboard. Although they provide something to hang on to in an emergency, they do lack the good solid feel of a proper handhold which is strong enough to take your full weight. Guard rails are also generally placed too low to allow comfortable movement when holding on to them. To be really effective they would need to be placed at waist height, which would detract from the appearance of the boat; they would also require stanchions which would have to be firmly braced down to the deck to make them rigid enough, and this in turn would obstruct free movement around the deck.

Most guard rails have the top wire about two feet above the deck, with a second wire between this and deck level. The wires are supported by stanchions at regular intervals. The stanchions are fitted close to the side of the boat, and can be vulnerable when going alongside, particularly where there is any overhang or movement in the water. If the stanchions are mounted rigidly to the deck and get knocked, then as well as sustaining damage themselves, they are liable to damage the deck. Some designs are aimed at introducing a point at the base of the stanchion where it will bend or break rather than damage the mounting point at the deck, the argument being that it is easier to fit a new stanchion than to repair the deck. However, the difficulty with this type of stanchion is making it sufficiently rigid so that the wire can be pulled tight, an absolute necessity if the life lines are to be effective.

The lifelines invariably terminate at rigid stainless steel pulpits and pushpits, forward and aft, which provide a solid anchor point for the wires and at the same time a firm support for the crew working in these areas. The pulpit forward and the pushpit aft provide a safe structure to brace against when mooring the boat in harbour, and also provide a secure handhold when carrying out routine sail handling or anchoring operations. They also provide security in emergency situations such as towing. Similar sections of rigid tubing railing are sometimes fitted alongside the wheelhouse, making it easier and safer to negotiate past this area. Another place where a rigid tubular guard is sometimes fitted is on each side of the mast, giving the crew a positive support when working at the halyard winches or when reefing in this area. Whatever type of rails or lifelines are fitted, they should be strong and should not have any noticeable slack in them. To grab a slack lifeline when you are expecting it to be rigid can upset the balance more quickly than anything else, and the additional momentum which the slackness allows can make the chances of breaking or bending the stanchions that much greater.

One way of improving the practicality of guard rails or lifelines is to combine them with bulwarks. Bulwarks can help to increase the reserve buoyancy by allowing the hull to become more deeply immersed before water comes over the top, but such reserves rapidly disappear when the water does come over the top to fill the deck space. Then the water trapped on the deck can have a very negative effect on stability, and can also generate a free surface effect whereby all the water trapped on deck will run to one side with an additional surge effect when the vessel rolls. When bulwarks are fitted there must therefore be adequate draining arrangements. These can be provided by leaving gaps; by cutting holes between the bulwarks and the deck to allow water to drain away freely; or by having no bulwarks at all in the lowest part of the deck amidships. Primarily bulwarks are incorporated into motor sailers for aesthetic reasons: they visually alter the sheer line, adding to the boat's traditional look, and giving it a tidier external appearance. On most motor sailers the bulwarks are unlikely to be more than a foot or so deep; their use tends to be generally restricted to the motor orientated type of motor sailer, reflecting their fishing vessel origins. Where bulwarks are fitted they usually have a single wire lifeline above, which helps to produce a more secure arrangement because of the shorter stanchions.

Drainage and safety

Any motor sailer cockpit should be self-draining so that water cannot be permanently trapped in this area. These drains can go directly into the bilges which in turn can be pumped out, but this is not a particularly good idea as the water is still on board. It is much better to get rid of the water straight away over the side. This means having the cockpit sole above the waterline and fitting adequate size drains between the cockpit sole and the outside of the hull. These drains should be of sufficient size to get rid of the water quickly; a 2 in pipe is normally adequate for this purpose. The drain from the port side of the cockpit should run across

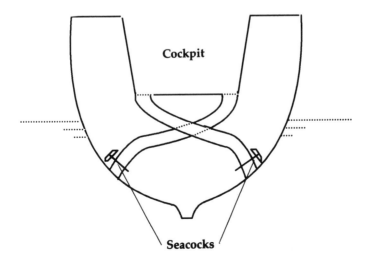

FIG 28   Cockpit drains led to the opposite side of the hull so that water does not run back up the drain when the boat is heeled.

and exit the hull on the starboard side, whilst the starboard drain should exit on the port side of the hull, an arrangement which helps to prevent water running back up the drain pipes when the vessel is heeled. A large cockpit can hold a ton or more of water, and it is not difficult to imagine the effect of such an additional weight on the stability. The extra weight also lowers the boat bodily into the water, which in turn increases the chance of another wave coming on board, thereby compounding the problem. Solid water like this in the cockpit can put considerable strain on the doors or washboards which offer the protection between the wet outside and the dry inside of the wheelhouse or the accommodation. On a wide cockpit, the free surface effect can be a compounding problem as well, not only upsetting the stability but also increasing the chance of further solid water coming on board from subsequent waves. Unless water can be cleared from a cockpit quickly and efficiently in rough conditions, shipping a green wave could lead to serious difficulties.

By their very nature, motor sailers tend to be used by serious cruising sailors. This means that they must be able to cope with heavy weather conditions. If a craft is to operate safely in these conditions, then the design must be such as to minimise the chance of any water finding its way down inside the hull. After all, one of the main functions of the deck and superstructure is to keep water out, and ideally the access to the inside of the hull should be watertight. However, achieving full water-tightness can be expensive and often inconvenient, making life on board uncomfortable. Once more, a sensible compromise has to be reached.

Wheelhouse doors and cockpit locker hatches should all be reasonably well fitting and, perhaps more importantly, strong enough to stand up to the impact of waves. Doors which can open up to give good access into the cockpit from the wheelhouse may need to be assessed for their suitability in this respect, and there may be a need to double them up with washboards or other protection when caught out in rough seas. The cockpit lockers are another area where water could find its way below; the hatches here should be reasonably watertight and the lids be capable of being secured so that they will not open or float off if the cockpit gets flooded. Engine hatches which may open up directly into the floor of the cockpit should be similarly treated.

A totally enclosed wheelhouse provides an intermediate barrier between the sea outside and the accommodation down below. In trying to keep the water on one side and dry comfort on the other, a motor sailer owner should decide where his first line of defence is going to be. The choice is between the outer wheelhouse door and the whole wheelhouse structure, and the inner access to the accommodation. The answer to this would appear to be obvious – and if it were only the outside door which had to be made water resistant then the solution would be quite simple – but wheelhouses on many motor sailers have large areas of glass to give good visibility all round, and it is these which could be vulnerable in rough weather. Certainly the forward facing windows of the windscreen should be made from toughened glass, and it is best if the same material is used for the side windows. However, the toughened glass is only as good as the frames in which it is mounted, and the whole wheelhouse structure should be strongly built from good material if it is to cope with keeping water outside in rough conditions.

It is to be hoped that a fully enclosed wheelhouse would usually be a dry area in the boat, but there will inevitably be a certain amount of damp and wet entering the wheelhouse. It could be necessary to have a window open to get good visibility in bad conditions which could let in damp and wet, or it might simply come from wet oilskins brought inside. Either way, the interior finish and furnishings should be able to stand up to this amount of water. The main sufferer from any damp or water getting in, though, is likely to be the electrical and electronic equipment. It can make sense to mount this high up in the wheelhouse to keep it out of the way of any water which may be flying about, but of course the sensible solution if you suspect that damp may be a problem is to invest in high quality waterproof equipment, both electronic and electrical, so that the water doesn't create problems. With the prospect of water coming into the wheelhouse area a small drain fitted on either side of the wheelhouse deck could take the water clear and drain it into the bilges.

Visibility

Visibility is important for safety and, whilst on many motor sailers there is the option of steering from an outside position, visibility from inside the wheelhouse should also be carefully considered. An enclosed wheelhouse does restrict visibility, and certainly it should be possible to open windows when necessary. A forward opening window can be very useful in fog, and one window on each side should also be capable of being opened, both to get ventilation in warm weather and also to improve the visibility at night time or in other deteriorating conditions. Vision at night is affected by lights in the wheelhouse which reflect against the windows; all lights on the dashboard or in other parts of the wheelhouse should therefore be capable of being switched off or covered. This particularly applies to indicator lights on radios and other electronic equipment. The angled windows favoured by many work boats can greatly enhance night-time visibility by cutting down on reflections; these are favoured on some motor orientated motor sailers and make for a very practical arrangement which also helps maximise the space in the wheelhouse.

In any enclosed steering position, or any area where the helmsman has to look through glass, windscreen wipers should be considered to be essential. These need to be reliable, robust and designed for marine use. Combining the wipers with fresh water windscreen washers is also a useful feature, because in conditions of light spray the wipers will simply smear the salt water on the screen.

The open steering position certainly gives good visibility, unless

The reverse sloping wheelhouse windows on this motor sailer will reduce reflections at night. Note the Dorade-style ventilators, the non-skid surface on the coachroof and the large sliding hatch in the wheelhouse roof.

restricted by masts or sails. Many motor sailer users prefer the open steering position because they like to see what is happening with the sails when they are in use, particularly when sailing the boat close-hauled. Enclosed wheelhouses are often fitted with windows in the roof or top of the shelter to bring the mainsail into view. Obviously such windows cannot provide the same clear view as from an open steering position, but they can be adequate and are often combined with hatches which can be opened in fine weather to improve ventilation. Another alternative is to fit a large sliding hatch, rather like the sunroof on a car, which can be slid back in fine weather to convert an enclosed wheelhouse into a semi-open steering position. However, such sliding hatches are not always easy to keep fully watertight and need to be carefully engineered if they are to be successful.

The question of good visibility cannot be over-emphasised both for collision avoidance in all weathers and for watching the sea in bad weather. One often hears yachtsmen criticising 'big ships' for not keeping a good lookout and for not being aware of small craft in their vicinity, but the same accusation could be made against many yachtsmen. With an enclosed wheelhouse there can often be blind spots between window pillars and other areas, and it is not unusual to find the view astern partially blocked, a potential danger on a vessel with the comparatively slow speed of a motor sailer, since many faster craft could be coming up astern unnoticed.

Wheelhouse interior

Many hours will be spent in the wheelhouse or wheel shelter whilst on passage. In harbour, too, the crew tend to congregate in the wheelhouse as it offers a good view of what is going on around the boat. Seating is an important consideration, therefore. It can be very tiring standing all the time on passage, so certainly the helmsman deserves a seat. A comfortable seat will allow him to pay full attention to controlling the boat, rather than spending half his time just trying to hang on; one with arm rests will help to locate him securely when the boat is rolling about in bad weather. A seat belt can also be very beneficial, to take some of the strain away from holding on, and a well placed footrest will allow the helmsman to brace against the pitching and rolling of the boat; this in turn helps to prevent fatigue. The steering wheel can then be used for controlling the boat, rather than as a handhold as is the case when standing at the wheel.

It is usual to find a vertical steering wheel used in a motor sailer. This conforms with sail boat practice, but does not always give the optimum method of controlling the boat. A vertical wheel is fine when standing at the steering position but it can be difficult when seated to find somewhere to park your knees without interfering with the movement of the wheel. Although some might feel that this is moving too much towards powerboat practice, an angled steering wheel can actually provide a satisfactory solution to this problem. For steering a boat for long periods from the seated position, it certainly provides the best and most efficient arrangement. Tilting steering wheels are now available, the angle of which can be adjusted through about 30 degrees.

Whilst the seating for the helmsman is of paramount importance, seating for the rest of the crew should also be considered. Here we come up against another area of conflict in motor sailer design. Because the wheelhouse is often the social area when in harbour, there will often be comfortable settees provided. However, these tend to be far from comfortable at sea when the boat is moving about, and do not always give a view of the outside world, something which the crew will appreciate. Individual seating, preferably facing fore and aft, is a much better arrangement. Ideally, each of the crew should be provided with a seat similar to that of the helmsman; if these seats swivel then they can also meet the requirements for socialising when the boat is in harbour. Unfortunately in modern motor sailer design it is invariably settees which are fitted, and the crew have to make do with what they have got!

A seatbelt is a good idea on any seating which is going to be used at sea, even if it is only a lap strap. This prevents the occupant of the seat being thrown about if the boat moves violently, reducing the risk of injury, and also allows the occupant to relax, instead of having to concentrate on holding on and bracing the whole time. If the crew are going to enjoy their time at sea, then adequate seating and good handholds are a must. There is nothing more tiring than trying to hold on to a seat which has inadequate handholds, and on a long passage this can put quite a strain on the crew.

Handholds and security

When seats cannot be provided due to lack of space, then good hand-holds are still necessary. Not only must they be adequate and strong, but they must also be in the right places. New boats are, in the main, poorly equipped with handholds; many of those which are fitted cannot always be gripped properly due to poor design or location. The trend seems to be appearance first and function second, and it is often left to the owner to fit his own handholds – though at least then he can put them in the right place. It is worth spending some time in finding the right places for handholds, because they can make such a tremendous difference to the comfort of life on board when at sea; they also make moving about much safer. One of the best types for the wheelhouse is a vertical pole in the centre of the wheelhouse which can be both held and leant against, but such a pole does hinder free passage unless the open space is quite large.

Alternatively handholds can be fitted to the roof or sides of the wheelhouse. Handholds on the dashboard, and adjacent to companion-ways and doors, can also be vital for safe movement about the boat, and for use when operating electronic equipment in the wheelhouse. Hand-holds on deck are equally important. With any handhold it is important that you can get your hand right round the grip for a secure hold. In designing and placing handholds it is worth remembering that strength is important, too: if the boat is moving about at all violently, a person can put a surprisingly high strain on a handhold in trying to prevent themselves being thrown around. A handhold which is not reliable is dangerous and trying, and careful attention needs to be paid to the fastenings.

The feet and legs can help a great deal in locating a person when moving about the deck. Although they cannot grip, feet and legs can be used to brace against the movement of the boat, and advantage should be taken of this. Bulwarks are very helpful on deck but, failing this, a toe rail is very useful to brace against movement. A toe rail is a raised edge to the deck and is a fairly standard finish. It is also helpful in preventing anything which may be dropped on the deck from sliding straight over the side.

Safety on deck can be greatly enhanced by a suitable non-slip deck covering. This is commonly fitted on motor sailers where there is a stronger emphasis on quality and practicality rather than appearance. Good deck coverings are both heavy and expensive, but the added security they give is well worth it. In the interests of economy, a covering is sometimes fitted only to the areas of deck most used. Alternatives are to mould in a roughened surface on a glass fibre deck moulding: this can work fairly well when the boat is new, but with age the rough surface gradually wears smooth, and of course the small indentations fill up with dirt and lose their attractive appearance. There is little that can be done to restore the roughness, except to cover the area with anti-slip covering. There are also special anti-slip paints available which can be applied to deck surfaces, although their useful life tends to be limited. Wooden decks are an attractive alternative, and the wood has a reasonable anti-slip property, but such decks do require a fair bit of maintenance if they are to retain their attractive appearance. For the owner spending a lot of time on board this may not be much of a problem but for the weekend sailor it can be a considerable burden.

Fuel and water fillers

One of the aspects which is important when considering the deck layout is the location of the fillers for both the fuel and the water tanks. These fillers should be slightly raised so that any water on the deck will not flow directly into the tanks. It goes without saying that there should be a watertight cap to both types of filler, and they should also be clearly labelled so that you don't mix the contents of the tanks. Although any overflow from the water tank when it is being filled is not significant, spillage from the fuel filler should be avoided at all costs, and the only really satisfactory way to do this is to have a specially constructed funnel which screws into the filler pipe. This will not only reduce the chances of spillage, but will also catch any fuel which is blown back up the pipe when the tank is nearly full and when the breather pipe may not be doing its job properly. Such a funnel also allows you to have water flowing on the deck during the refuelling operation so that any spillage is immediately washed away, although modern requirements in most ports and harbours prohibit any discharge of fuel overboard, so rags or absorbent paper should be available to absorb any spillage.

Water tank fillers are better placed at a higher location on the deck than the fuel fillers – and well away from them, so there is no chance of contamination should there be any fuel spillage. Fuel and water are often taken on board at the same time (and often in a hurry), and there should not be any chance of them mixing during this operation. The fuel filler is best placed at the lowest part of the deck with a scupper close by, so that any spillage will drain straight overboard, and any deck covering and its adhesive around the fuel filler should be as fuel-proof as possible. The fuel pipes used for supplying fuel to boats come in a wide variety of shapes and sizes, and so the filler opening should be as large as possible, bearing in mind that cruising yachts often have to use the same pipes and nozzles as working craft. Because of the possibility of using large fuel pipes, the breathing pipe must also be of adequate size to prevent blow backs in the filling pipe.

Hatches

In the interests of ventilation, and as a secondary exit from the accommo-dation below in the event of fire, a hatch is invariably fitted on the foredeck or in the forward end of the coachroof. Such a hatch also provides a quick method of getting head sails on or off the deck. This fore hatch is in an exposed position, and traditionally can be a constant source of leaks, although with modern design the problem of leaking has largely been solved. To meet the requirements of providing a fire escape, this hatch must be of adequate size and must be capable of being opened quickly and easily from the inside. Nothing should be stored on top of the hatch, certainly not a dinghy or other heavy equipment which might make it difficult to use this emergency exit. Modern hatches often have a large part of their area fitted with a clear plastic insert to give more light below, and metal bars are often fitted to protect this plastic area from impact and from being scratched when cleaning the deck or walking around. When there is an aft cabin, a similar hatch should be fitted there for escape purposes; this too can also serve as a ventilator.

Davits and a bathing platform attached to the transom of a steel motor sailer. Whilst these are practical features on a motor sailer they also increase the overall length which can mean increased marina charges.

Stowage

Stowage of equipment on deck can be quite a problem, particularly on smaller motor sailers. There may be a need to stow the dinghy on deck on longer passages; there is also the liferaft to consider, and things like the anchor and other items of equipment which cannot easily be stowed below. These will be looked at more closely in Chapter 10 on equipment. As far as the dinghy is concerned, these are now more frequently being stowed in davits mounted across the transom. This keeps the boat out of the way and leaves the deck space clear; it also helps to make the launch and recovery of the dinghy easy. If you get caught out in rough seas, however, the dinghy can be vulnerable stowed in this location. It is equally vulnerable if it is stored up on the coachroof or the wheelhouse top, and it tends to get in the way in these areas. It makes a lot of sense to have an inflatable dinghy which can be stowed away down below on longer passages. The liferaft needs to be readily available, so the options with this are to stow it on the coachroof or, as seems to be the modern practice, to have it stowed on a transom bracket. Certainly the transom bracket makes for easy launching in an emergency, but any stowage here needs to be very secure. Cockpit lockers are often used for stowing ropes and fenders, although fenders in particular can be very hard to stow inside lockers because they take up a lot of space. Once again the transom can be a useful space to stow fenders out of the way in specially constructed racks where they are still easily reachable.

Ventilation

The deck and superstructure have to accommodate windows and ventilators to provide light and air down below. In considering these it is important that the watertight integrity of the hull is maintained. Because the motor sailer is designed for operating in rough conditions, any windows or portholes should be small in area, strong in construction, and adequately fastened to the hull or deck. From a safety aspect, windows should be of the non-opening type, but this often conflicts with the requirements for ventilation; so if they do open, there should be means of securing them tightly when at sea. All windows should have a metal frame in which they are securely supported and secured to the hull, because any outside windows can be subject to considerable pressure when hit by a green sea. The trend towards large wheelhouse windows in motor sailers is certainly nice from the point of view of the crew inside, but these will be more susceptible to breakage through impact. All external windows should be of toughened glass to help reduce this risk. As far as ventilators are concerned, these should be capable of being blocked off to prevent any water entering the accommodation. They should also be strong enough to withstand a solid wave sweeping across the deck. (See Fig 29 on page 126.)

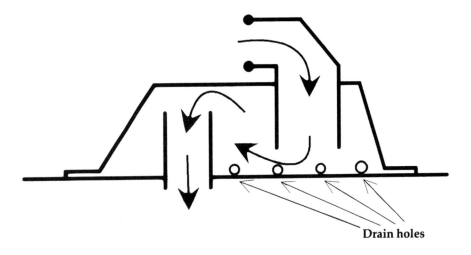

Drain holes

FIG 29   A Dorade-type vent which allows air to enter the interior of the boat in bad weather, whilst any water mixed with the air drains off through the drain holes.

Safety

There has been considerable emphasis on safety in this chapter: too much, you may think. However, it is as well to remember that motor sailers are capable of – and often used on – extended sea passages, and are thus more likely to meet all sorts of weather conditions without the benefit of shelter near at hand. Motor sailers tend to be designed to operate in severe conditions, and safety at sea largely depends on attention to detail. It is rare that main structures, such as the hull, fail at sea, but it is far from rare for many of the smaller fixtures and fittings around the deck to fail. Whilst this in itself may not be too serious, one failure can start a chain reaction which can lead to dangerous situations. Safety is largely a personal thing, and it is up to each owner to decide on his own level of safety when he goes to sea, but he also has a responsibility towards his crew. It is in the deck and superstructure areas that many of the potential components at risk are located, and their vulnerability should be carefully considered.

CHAPTER 9

━━━━━

ACCOMMODATION

One of the major developments which has taken place in recent years in motor sailer design has been the ability to make better use of the available space down below. A comparison between motor sailers of 20 years ago and modern designs shows a dramatic increase in the amount of accommodation which has been fitted inside a hull of a given length. Not all of this improvement can be attributed to better internal design, however. A great deal of the improvement comes in the way that hull design has changed: modern motor sailers tend to have much fuller lines. The beam of the hull has expanded outwards and there is usually a greater depth of hull, whilst superstructures have also been raised so that a great deal more space is created inside the hull. This in turn allows the designer greater freedom to provide all the comforts of home on a modern motor sailer.

In trying to fit in as much accommodation as possible, considerable ingenuity has been used in many modern designs. Seats convert into sleeping berths, tables in the saloon sometimes have to double up as chart tables, galley work surfaces may also be covers over the sink or storage areas. Having this type of dual function is an arrangement which can work reasonably well in harbour when the boat is not moving around and where there is usually time and space to sort things out, but at sea it can make life very difficult: the inconvenience of changing an item from one use to another is not recommended for comfortable cruising. One of the guiding features of motor sailer accommodation should be that any need to alter or adapt the accommodation to meet different roles should be kept to the bare minimum. This is particularly important on smaller motor sailers.

Crew numbers

Although boat length is still a measure of the way yachts are categorised, it is becoming increasingly common to judge yachts by the number of sleeping berths which have been incorporated. Whilst a six berth 30 footer could be considered to be an advanced design simply because the designer has managed to squeeze six berths into this compact overall

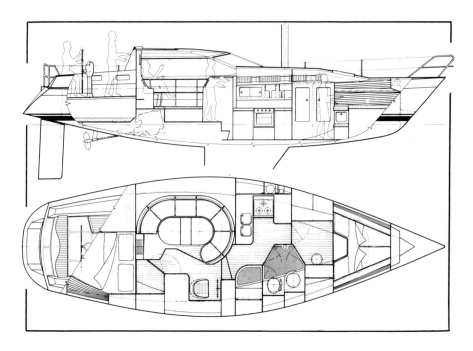

FIG 30   Layout of a typical motor sailer with a low profile wheelhouse. This is very much a sailing orientated version with the emphasis on the open sailing cockpit. Note the double berth under the cockpit which has very restricted headroom.

length, and the number of berths available on board can be a useful yardstick in gauging the capacity of a motor sailer, in reality six berths on a 30 footer would put a very heavy premium on the available space, and the boat is not likely to be particularly comfortable to live aboard when all the berths are occupied. Squeezing in additional berths is one thing, but there are other considerations to take into account, such as stowage of personal belongings for the crew members, eating and toilet facilities, and adequate space in the wheelhouse. Squeezing in extra berths can also put pressure on the stowage required for sails, fenders and other equipment. The fact that designers go to such great lengths to fit in as many berths as possible does suggest that many people buy boats largely with the objective of providing accommodation when alongside in the marina. Six berths in a 30 footer could be acceptable when alongside, but with a full crew on board at sea in a moderate breeze, it could be absolute hell!

A motor sailer is a yacht intended for comfortable and reliable cruising. Comfort on a long passage demands enough space to move about, and to stow personal belongings as well as all the yacht's equipment. At sea, it should be possible for the whole crew to be in the wheelhouse or the cockpit at one time without being cramped, because this is where everyone will tend to congregate. Few people enjoy being down below at sea unless they are sleeping or are having to cook. Judging the accommodation of a yacht simply by the number of berths is therefore not very realistic. Unless the same numbers can be accommodated with a considerable degree of comfort in the other social areas on board, then the number of berths is irrelevant. The space in the wheelhouse would be a much better yardstick by which to judge the capacity of a motor sailer.

As a general rule, then, a yardstick of one person for every 10 feet of the length would be a good guide to gauging the maximum crew for comfortable cruising. This gives a three person crew on a 30 footer, which sounds about right, both in terms of comfort and in handling the boat. If this measure is borne in mind when choosing a boat there will not be too much disappointment. Another method is simply to count the permanent berths on board: the same 30 footer would probably allow four permanent berths, the others being convertible seats, which is a much better capacity level for such a craft. Counting only permanent berths is also much more realistic, because converting the seats in the saloon into sleeping berths at night never really works out very well in practice. By keeping to the permanent sleeping berths and leaving the saloon areas in their day-time state, you end up with a much happier and more practical layout arrangement for comfortable cruising.

Berths

The requirements for sleeping berths when they are used at sea and in harbour are sometimes conflicting. It is now common to find the master sleeping berth being equipped as a comfortable double bed, which is a fine arrangement where a couple own the boat. In harbour a double berth is a splendid idea, allowing connubial bliss whilst saving space as well, but at sea when the boat may be rolling or heeling over in one direction, there is little to stop you sliding about, and sleeping can be a fitful experience. If you sail without your partner, such a double berth tends to be a very impractical idea, unless you are on extremely good terms with the person you are sharing with. The movement of the boat is likely to guarantee that neither of you gets much sleep; with such an arrangement it is almost impossible to fit up leeboards or other features which reduce the risk of being thrown about at sea.

Even many modern single berths fitted on motor sailers are not always very practical for use at sea. Tiered bunks are impractical, and the use of permanent leeboards which project above the level of the mattress and make an edge to the berth has fallen out of fashion, as such berths cannot be easily used as seats. Temporary boards or canvas can be used as an alternative, but these still have to be stored out of the way in harbour when not in use. A modern solution to providing a secure berth at sea tends to be the use of webbing straps which extend from the outer edge of the berth to the deck head or to the side of the boat. These will stop you falling out of the berth, but they will not necessarily prevent you

The aft cabin on a modern 40 footer showing the large double bed which is a feature in the master cabin of many designs. *Photo: Nauticat*

from rolling about, and you cannot jam your body into position as you can with leeboards. The other option, of course, if straps or leeboards are not fitted, is to use the berths on the lee side of the hull when the yacht is heeled over, and here you are much less likely to fall out because you are firmly located in the 'V' formed between the back of the berth and the mattress.

It is when you are at sea that berths such as the settee seats can prove quite valuable for getting sleep, particularly when they are on the lee side. Quarter berths can be another favourite place at sea, although these have also fallen out of fashion because the space they used to occupy can be put to better use. At sea at least some of the crew will have to be on watch, so that a couple of good, practical berths which can be used when the boat is moving about will probably suffice. These could compensate for the disadvantages found with the large double berths.

Apart from the considerations of privacy and convenience, the position of berths on board a motor sailer is not particularly important when

Securing straps

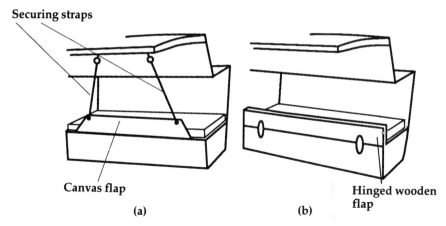

Canvas flap

(a)

Hinged wooden flap

(b)

FIG 31   Alternative arrangements for bunk lee boards. (a) shows a canvas flap attached to the bunk base and secured in place by the webbing straps attached to the deck head. (b) is a hinged wooden flap which is secured upright by bolts at either end of the bunk.

the yacht is in harbour. At sea, however, berths in the bow and stern can be subject to a considerable amount of movement when the boat is pitching and pounding, and this can make them uncomfortable or even untenable. The double beds are usually located in the bow or the stern, which tends to make them doubly unsuitable for use at sea. Berths in the bow can be particularly subject to quite large vertical movements: this can be very noticeable when a boat is beating to windward. Berths in the stern or in the quarter tend to be more comfortable, but the snag here is that you are much more susceptible to propeller and engine noise if you are motor sailing. This makes the availability of a couple of good single berths, located somewhere near the centre of the boat, an important feature for use at sea if the watch down below are to get a degree of comfort. The saloon berths can provide a very viable alternative sleeping area at sea, offering both comfort and security.

Handholds

There is a disturbing tendency in modern motor sailer design to ignore the requirements for comfortable living when at sea. This not only applies to the sleeping arrangements but also extends to facilities such as handholds, required for moving safely about the boat at sea. As discussed in Chapter 8, these are vital in the wheelhouse and on deck, but are also important down below, where it can be difficult to anticipate the movement of the boat. Handholds should be located so that there is something to hold on to all the time when moving around inside the boat. You even need suitable handholds for when you are getting dressed, or at least a means of locating yourself so you don't get thrown about. It is vital to avoid any injury to the crew, and any handholds which are fitted should, therefore, be both well constructed and adequately fastened.

Headroom

Apart from the sleeping berths which take up a lot of the available space inside the hull, room also has to be found for cooking facilities, a toilet area, somewhere to eat, and stowage of the items of loose equipment, both large and small, which are vital to the operation of the boat. There should also be room for navigation, and there is no real substitute for a dedicated chart table for this purpose. Headroom is an important consideration in most of these areas, but particularly so in the galley and toilet area if contortions are to be avoided. Full headroom usually means about 6 ft 3 in, and you will need this in all the main areas where you will be moving around the boat. Good headroom is usually found along the centreline of the boat, where the cabin sole is deepest and there is a coachroof to increase the height, but the galley and toilet areas are often placed on one side of the boat, and here there can be considerable problems with headroom, particularly if the design incorporates a coachroof.

Galley

Cooking facilities on cruising yachts have changed considerably from the time when a single burner, alcohol or paraffin stove was considered adequate. Cruising yachtsmen now demand all the comforts of home when they go to sea, and this extends to the provision of not only a cooking stove complete with oven, but also a refrigerator and running water at the sink. These sophisticated facilities will mainly be used in harbour, but bearing in mind that motor sailers should be designed for extended cruising, then the galley needs to be designed to be suitable for use at sea. Anyone who is brave enough to prepare meals at sea deserves special consideration, and they certainly deserve the best possible facilities to make the job as easy, quick and pleasant as possible. Meals at sea on a long passage are very important from a morale point of view, but can be difficult to produce if the boat is tossing about. It is not unknown to see the cook produce a splendid meal at sea and then be unable to eat it because he or she has been shut up for too long down below preparing it, and the spectre of seasickness has caught up.

Ideally the galley, if it is located below, should be placed somewhere close to the companionway into the wheelhouse, so that the cook has some communication with the outside world. This also means that food can be passed up easily into the wheelhouse, if this is the designated eating area. One disadvantage of having the galley located close to the wheelhouse in this way is that steam from the cooking process can mist up the wheelhouse windows, reducing visibility. The solution here is adequate ventilation.

A difficult galley for use at sea, where the fridge door could interfere with the stove, and the chopping board cover to the stove could be a nuisance.

If a large enclosed wheelhouse is fitted, then it is possible to install the galley inside it. This is a trend which can be seen on some motor cruisers, particularly those of Scandinavian origin, and there is no reason why it shouldn't be extended to motor sailers. There are many advantages in having the galley in this location, both in harbour and at sea. There are drawbacks, though, particularly the steam misting up the wheelhouse windows, and it does take up a valuable part of what is considered the premium space on board. Some owners may also feel that having the galley in the wheelhouse means that when visitors come on board it is like taking them into their house through the kitchen or back door. One solution here may be to have a compromise arrangement, whereby a small microwave cooker or an electric kettle can be installed in the wheelhouse, leaving the main galley down below. Certainly, if meals are prepared at sea, then either a microwave or an electric kettle can be very valuable items of equipment, providing simple meals without the necessity of going down below. With modern heavy duty alternators they can be a practical fitting which will not put too heavy a drain on the boat's batteries, particularly when the engine is running.

The key point of any galley is the stove, and there are three main types which are used. Gas stoves using butane or propane gas are probably the easiest to use, and can now come with automatic ignition systems so that as the valve is opened the gas lights. However, some countries will not allow this type of stove to be installed below decks because of the attendant fire risks should there be a leak in the gas system. The gases are heavier than air and will sink into the bilges; when mixed with air they can form an explosive mixture which can be detonated by a spark from an electric switch or the hot exhaust at the engine. Gas detectors are available which will indicate the presence of gas in the bilges, and these should be considered an essential fitting if gas is installed on board. Because the gas is heavier than air, ventilation is not adequate to remove the gas, and if leaks are detected then some sort of forced draft system should be used to clear the gas from the bilges. Do not, however, employ one which uses an electric fan with exposed contacts, since this might create the spark necessary for ignition. Gas cylinders should be stowed in separate compartments which are sealed so that the gas cannot leak into the bilges from this compartment, and there should be drains fitted which will direct any leaking gas overboard. The gas cylinders should be turned off when not in use and the piping needs to be carefully installed and checked for leaks at regular intervals using soapy water. This will bubble if leaks exist. Another form of gas cylinder uses high pressure gas which is lighter than air. This is becoming popular in the USA and its use will no doubt spread. The advantages of this gas are, firstly, that the cylinder can be fitted with a pressure gauge to show how much gas is left and, secondly, the gas is much safer because any leakage will rise and disperse through the hatches or doors.

The problems with gas cookers mean that paraffin stoves are still used on some motor sailers. These days they are comparatively easy to use and reasonably odourless compared with some of their predecessors. The problem with paraffin stoves is that there is a delay between switching on and being ready for cooking, and whilst this is not too inconvenient in harbour, it can prove a nuisance at sea. Fuel is comparatively cheap, readily obtainable, and reasonably safe, but with kerosene cookers it is less easy to get grill and oven facilities, so that kerosene stoves tend to be used only where extensive cooking is not a prime requirement.

Alcohol stoves are an alternative which find favour on many cruising boats, particularly in those countries where bottled gas stoves are not permitted. Alcohol burns with a clean, hot flame and is not explosive. Grills and ovens can be incorporated using this fuel, although the fuel itself tends to be more expensive than the alternatives.

The other option is to use an electric cooker, though whilst a micro-wave cooker can operate off the boat's battery system (even though the drain is fairly heavy), full-blown electric cookers similar to those found in houses can only be used if the boat is plugged into a shore supply, or if there is a reasonable size of mains generator on board. Certainly electric cooking is wonderfully convenient, particularly when you are at sea, but because of the need for a generator, the use of electric stoves tends to be restricted to the larger types of motor sailer.

Refrigerators can run off the boat's battery system, but this is only viable if the engine is running for most of the time, otherwise the drain on the battery can be unacceptable. If a suitable generator is fitted, or shore power supply available, then the larger domestic sizes of refrigerator, or even a deep freeze, can be run. Refrigerators are available which can operate from different voltages, so that they can be switched to the mains shore supply in harbour and run off the boat's batteries at sea, whilst other designs of refrigerator can also operate on gas as well as an electrical supply. Refrigerators are available as complete units ready for installation or can come as just the refrigeration unit, which is installed in a purpose-designed, insulated box which can double up as an ice box. There are plenty of options when it comes to refrigerators, both in terms of size and fuel, and refrigerators now tend to be considered as essential items of equipment on board motor sailers.

The sink is also considered indispensable. In most modern designs it is fitted with both hot and cold running water to give most of the convenience of home. Water systems which pressurise the water flow by means of an electric pump are now commonly fitted, and these tend to operate with a pressurised tank. The water starts flowing as soon as the tap is opened, with the pump switching in to restore pressure when this has dropped below a pre-set level. Such an arrangement does put a drain on the batteries, which is fine when the engine is running, but when at anchor overnight can, along with the demands of the refrigerator and the lighting system, overstrain the system. The noise of the electric water pump can also be an irritant at night if it switches on at intervals to maintain the pressure, but that can easily be solved by switching it off at the main.

Heating hot water for domestic requirements can be done by two main methods. The same bottled gas that is used for cooking can be used to fuel a water heater which lights automatically when the hot tap is turned on, heating only the water as it is needed. This is a similar arrangement to that found in many domestic gas heaters, but it does extend the risks of using gas in an enclosed area. Kerosene and alcohol fuels are not particularly suited for water heating because they are not automatic, although in some installations where a heating system for the accommodation runs on diesel fuel, this can also be adapted to combine it with water heating. However, the main option to heating water with bottled gas is to use the engine cooling system. This is linked up to an insulated tank, which in turn is connected to the domestic water system. The heat from the engine cooling system heats the water in the calorifier tank through coils which are fitted inside the tank. Of course such a system will only work when the engine is running, although the insulation fitted around the tank will keep the water hot for a considerable time after the

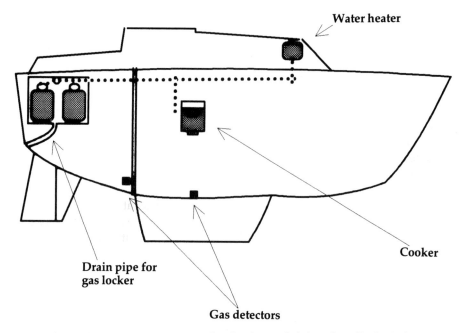

Water heater

Cooker

Drain pipe for
gas locker

Gas detectors

FIG 32 A typical gas system on a motor sailer. Gas is supplied via a shut-off valve to the cooker and water heater using copper pipe. A flexible link will be required if the cooker is gimballed. The drain pipe allows any leaking gas in the gas locker to drain overboard, and the gas detectors give early warning of any leakage.

engine has been shut down. The calorifier tank is often fitted with an electric immersion heater which is powered by the shore supply when the boat is alongside in the marina, and this caters for the harbour hot water requirements, but under sail you have to rely on the stored hot water with no means of replenishing it except by running the engine.

If a galley is going to be adequate for producing good meals it can take up quite a bit of the space inside the accommodation, but this tends to be acceptable in modern motor sailer designs. Like the rest of the accommodation, there is a tendency for the galley to be designed more for use in harbour than at sea. For serious cruising, quite a lot of thought is necessary to make the galley a viable proposition at sea. You need some means of securing pots and pans on to the stove to prevent them sliding around through the movement of the boat, and working surfaces should at least have a lip around the edge to stop equipment sliding off. In addition to stopping pans sliding off the stove, a useful feature is a cup rack, which can hold cups while hot liquids are being poured into them, though these are the sort of features that an owner can incorporate into the galley himself. Space should be provided for the stowage of pots and pans, cutlery, and all the other requirements of cooking, and plenty of lockers are required for stowing food. These should be designed so that if the boat is rolling at sea, the contents don't spill out when the door is opened.

Toilet compartment

Whilst the galley seems to be allocated plenty of space in modern designs, the same cannot always be said of the toilet compartment. Here the designer is often trying to fit a toilet, wash basin and a shower into a space less than 3 feet square, and even where there is adequate floor area there is not always adequate headroom. Using the shower will tend to make everything else in the toilet compartment wet, which is not a particularly good arrangement, but it is another of the compromises that have to be made on smaller motor sailers. In many recent designs, more attention is being paid to the toilet compartment facilities, and these may now incorporate a separate shower compartment or a separate compartment for the WC. On larger craft where space is less at a premium, not only can the toilet facilities be more adequate, but there may even be two compartments, one forward and one aft, to integrate with the individual sleeping compartments, giving the sort of luxury which is now being demanded.

Organising the services and facilities in the toilet compartment has improved considerably in many modern motor sailer designs, so that the compartment really becomes comfortable to use both at sea and in harbour. At sea it will probably only be the toilet which is used, except perhaps on a long passage, and there should be adequate handholds in this area. The hot and cold water services are the same as those which supply the galley, but it is in getting rid of waste that problems tend to develop. The wash basin can usually drain directly overboard, because it is usually well above the outside waterline. However, this is not the case with the shower, so that the shower tray has to incorporate a pump which automatically comes on when the shower is switched on, and serves to pump the waste water up and over the side. Some showers will drain into the bilges where the bilge pump can be used to pump the waste water overboard, but this is not a particularly satisfactory arrangement, and can lead to nasty smells unless strict cleanliness is observed.

Few countries now allow raw sewage to be pumped overboard, so the options with the toilet are either to provide a holding tank where the waste can be stored until it can be pumped out alongside in harbour or in the marina using special facilities to remove the stored wastes, or to use a chemical toilet, although here again the waste still has to be removed in harbour. Such chemical toilets can be provided with an electric circulation system, similar to those used on aircraft, which helps to flush the toilet in a reasonably civilised manner, but the holding tank tends to be the favoured option in most modern designs. It is permissible in some areas to pump out the contents of the holding tank at sea, provided that this is done via a macerator which converts the wastes into semi-liquid form.

Attention needs to be paid to ventilation in both the toilet compartment and the galley. Ventilation used to be a vital feature of motor

A compact toilet compartment incorporating shower, WC and wash basin. The modern trend is to allocate more space and to place the WC and shower in individual compartments.

sailer design in the days of boats built of wood, where lack of ventilation could lead to rot in the timber structure. With most modern designs being built in glass fibre, ventilation is not so critical in this regard, but it can still be important for removing smells and preventing condensation. Ventilation is also vital in warmer climates to reduce the build up of heat and, in its simplest form, opening windows or ports can do the job. The escape hatches fitted to cabins can also be very useful here, except when it is raining, and the critical galley and toilet areas are often fitted with supplementary ventilation which can maintain a circulation of air through these compartments even when it is wet outside. Such ventilators can incorporate an electric fan, or can simply rely on the passing wind to do the job. It can be beneficial to have some form of ventilation on board for use when the boat has to be battened down against the elements, whether at sea or in harbour, and this can be useful when the shower is in use, or when there is serious cooking going on in the galley, which can cause heavy condensation in the boat and create the sort of damp atmosphere which can be very unpleasant on board.

Heating and air-conditioning

Motor sailers are designed for year-round use, so there can be times when heating is required, and times when air-conditioning could be of benefit. The need for air-conditioning is less likely, simply because any yachtsman sailing in warm conditions is more likely to opt for an open cockpit than an enclosed wheelhouse. However air-conditioning to keep the accommodation cool in harbour can be welcome, and here it can run off the shore supply. Most boat air-conditioners need a cooling water supply which can be taken from the engine sea water cooling system.

Heating is much more of a necessity for any motor sailer owner seeking to extend his sailing season, and here there is a choice of installations. Probably the best and most flexible arrangement is an independent heater operating off the same diesel fuel used by the engine. This tends to provide heat in the form of hot air which can be ducted around to the various compartments in the motor sailer, and particularly into the wheelhouse, with ducts below the windscreen to prevent the screen misting up. It is possible for such heaters to incorporate water heating as well, although in general this is kept separate from the space heating system. Another option is to use engine heat, with the engine cooling system being linked to a heat exchanger where a fan blows air over the heating grid, generating hot air which can then be ducted around the vessel. The snag here, of course, is that it only works when the engine is running, which makes the system far less flexible, particularly for harbour use. In a harbour with a mains power supply available, electric heaters can of course be used.

Various types of gas heater are available, of which the catalytic heater is probably the best and safest, although gas central heating systems are another option. Once again it is the possible explosion risk which can detract from the attractions of a gas system, although a well installed system with built-in safeguards can be safe for use. The value of a heating system in a motor sailer cannot be overestimated, and the ability to go cruising in the winter months with a large degree of comfort can greatly extend the pleasures of motor sailer ownership.

Layout

The internal layout of a motor sailer still tends towards the concept of having a sleeping cabin forward and the main saloon amidships. With the modern, deeper hull designs, space has been found to incorporate a second sleeping cabin aft, which may be under the wheelhouse or aft cockpit. This three cabin layout can make a very convenient arrangement, with internal access throughout the accommodation. One design trend which is attractive is the incorporation of the saloon and the wheelhouse – even though they are on different levels – in a type of open plan layout. In general interior yacht design is moving towards opening up the accommodation in this sort of way to give a feeling of spaciousness down below whilst still allowing for individual sleeping compartments to be closed off to give privacy. The galley and toilet compartments have now tended to be moved aft, fairly close to the forward end of the wheelhouse, which makes them much more convenient for use at sea, whilst the navigation space is now almost invariably and sensibly provided in the wheelhouse itself.

In considering any layout, convenience in harbour has to be balanced against practicality of use at sea, and ideally when people are asleep down below it should be possible to use the other facilities on board without disturbing the sleeping crew. The trend towards having an aft cabin is a spreading feature of motor sailer design, and it can be a practical arrangement. Access to the cabin from the wheelhouse is fine, but on larger motor sailer designs, a more satisfactory solution is to fit in an internal passageway between the saloon and the aft cabin around the edge of the motor compartment, which makes the wheelhouse space more usable as it becomes less of a passageway.

Furnishings

The traditional appearance of motor sailers is often carried through internally in the form of polished wooden panelling and fittings. Modern polished wood can be a practical and aesthetically pleasing finish to the interior of a motor sailer and, particularly when cruising in winter, generates a comfortable, cosy atmosphere. In warmer weather, though, such an interior can be somewhat claustrophobic, and if wood is still desired then lighter woods can give a greater feeling of space. A great deal can be done with the colour and textures of the various fabrics used internally for settees and curtains, and there is no doubt that the clever use of materials and clever design is responsible for the apparent spaciousness of many modern designs. With production motor sailers it is in this area of the accommodation that the owner probably has most scope to introduce personal touches. Pictures, books and ornaments can all help to create a particular atmosphere and dispel the feel of a mass-produced product. Having said that, the somewhat antiseptic atmosphere generated by GRP mouldings has largely disappeared from

This motor sailer wheelhouse has a dedicated area for navigation and radio communications which can make it much easier to use than trying to navigate on the saloon table.

modern motor sailer design, and the air of comparative luxury and comfort which has replaced it is largely due to a combination of a return to more traditional materials in modern form, and clever design which puts the emphasis on comfort and the illusion of space.

CHAPTER 10

───

EQUIPMENT

The amount of equipment on board a new motor sailer when it leaves the yard will vary greatly from builder to builder. However, unlike the days when yachts were supplied with just the basic equipment necessary to sail away, now modern motor sailers come equipped in most respects for extensive cruising. This change has come about largely because of greater integration in design. Every inch of space on board is now allocated for one function or another, which can leave an owner very little scope to add additional equipment or to make modifications. This means that either the designer has to do a complete job and make provision for all the requirements in the original design, or the owner has to adapt or change the craft in order to accommodate new items of equipment.

In some countries there are demands for specific items – such as safety equipment – to be incorporated into boats when supplied as new. Often, though, even large items such as a liferaft may not be supplied as standard, and an owner may find that he has to make provision for this to be installed when there is no obvious space left on board for stowing such a large item. The same goes for electronics, where there are still many options to meet specific cruising requirements options, and where the owner is left to make the decisions. Designers must grasp the fact that items such as radars, electronic charts and radios take up a lot of space, and space should be allocated for these in the original design. This is particularly relevant when the wheelhouse has to double up as a social area; in many designs the control area is squeezed into one corner leaving no room for expansion or additions. In this chapter we will be looking at the main items of equipment needed on board a motor sailer, including the various options available, and looking at where and how equipment should be stowed.

Safety equipment should obviously come somewhere near the top of the list of priorities when it comes to equipping a motor sailer. Builders tend to fit the bare minimum in terms of safety requirements, and there is always scope for improvement. The investment in safety equipment can be quite high, and at the end of the day it is, quite rightly, up to the owner to decide how much he wants to invest and what level of equipment, both in preventative and in emergency terms, is needed. Many countries demand a certain minimum which might include flares, lifejackets and fire extinguishers, but this is very much the minimum and it is rarely adequate to give a reasonable level of safety in practice.

Fire prevention

A fire at sea is a particularly frightening and dangerous experience and every care should be taken to avoid the situation. How to cope with fire if it does break out is covered in Chapter 11, but here we shall look at some of the fire prevention measures that can be taken and at firefighting equipment. There are four main areas where fire is likely to start: the accommodation, the galley, the engine compartment and the electrical circuits. Fire in the accommodation is most likely to be caused by smoking, so strict control of smoking on board and a discipline to ensure that lighted cigarette ends are not left around the boat will help to prevent this situation. In general, not much attention is paid to fireproofing boats, particularly in terms of the fittings and furnishings installed on board, and these could quickly add fuel to a fire. In the galley there are always risks where flame exists, and the galley should never be left unattended when something is cooking on the stove. In the small confines of the average yacht galley, it may also be necessary to reach over the stove to pick up utensils, which could set clothing on fire, so particular care should be taken here.

Electrical circuits probably provide the greatest hazard on board modern yachts, partly because they are hidden out of sight, and you can't see what is going on. The risk here comes from short-circuits which generate heat and sparks; these risks will be higher on metal craft, where any break in the insulation could earth the circuit. All electrical circuits should be protected by fuses or breakers which will greatly reduce the chance of fire if a circuit does prove faulty because they isolate that particular circuit automatically. One of the main fire risk areas is in the heavy duty battery cables, which are not protected by fuses or breakers; these need to be very carefully installed and maintained, as do the batteries themselves if the risk of fire is to be minimised.

In the engine compartment, apart from the electrical risks, it is the fuel which is the greatest danger. Some means of isolating the fuel tanks from outside the engine compartment is important. In this way, any fire will not be fed by further fuel, and you will have some chance of coping.

If fire does break out, it is vital that its source is detected quickly. In the confines of a small boat, detecting a fire sounds easy and obvious, but with the modern, fully enclosed type of engine compartment, a fire here could remain undetected for some time. Even if, as is the case with many motor sailer designs, the helmsman is standing on top of the engine compartment, by the time he has felt the increase in heat and perhaps smelt the smoke, the fire could have gained a considerable hold down below. Indeed the first warning might be when the engine slows or

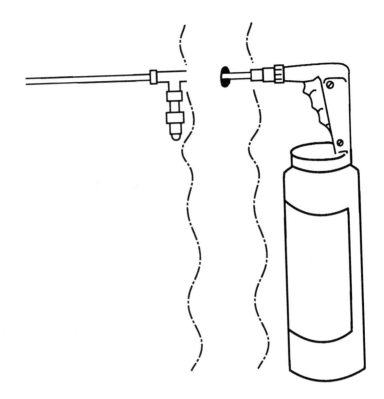

FIG 33   A fire extinguishing system for the engine compartment where the extinguisher is outside the compartment and connected by fixed piping and nozzles into the compartment. Such extinguishers can be made to discharge automatically or, in this case, they can be manually operated after a fire warning alarm at the dashboard has been activated.

stops. Such a machinery fire is only likely when the boat is proceeding under motor; the first indication of trouble is likely to be when the engine revolutions decrease for no apparent reason. The immediate reaction in such a situation is to open the engine hatches to find out what is wrong, but this action could immediately cause the fire to flare up and engulf the wheelhouse, creating a situation which could rapidly get out of hand. So an important piece of safety equipment is to have some means of fire detection or automatic extinguishing in the engine compartment. Smoke detectors are available, but tend to be a bit too sensitive. The most common installation is some form of heat plug which melts when a pre-set temperature level is reached. This can either be used to initiate a fire alarm at the helmsman's position, which then allows him to activate a permanent fire extinguishing system fitted into the engine compartment; or the warning system can be used to activate the extinguisher directly, providing what is in effect an automatic system. If such a system is to be fully successful, then it should be matched to some means of switching off any engine compartment fans from outside the compartment, and blanking off the air intakes and outlets, thereby starving this area of oxygen and allowing the fire extinguishing gas to do its job properly.

If a fire starts in the accommodation, there is a reasonable chance that it will be discovered in time to take action without the need for any fire detectors. Portable fire extinguishers are a standard means of dealing with such fires, and should be located throughout the accommodation. The fire extinguishers should be placed close to the exit of each compartment, preferably just outside, so that it is possible to grab the extinguisher and tackle the fire from a position of safety rather than having to go into the compartment to get it. A minimum requirement here should be one extinguisher for each compartment. Large and heavy fire extinguishers are not always the most practical for use at sea. If the boat is moving around a lot, then you may need one hand for holding on and one for operating the fire extinguisher, so that a smaller, compact unit can be better, although obviously they have a limited capacity, usually around 1 kg of liquid. The very small, hand-held extinguishers are not particularly satisfactory on board a boat because of their very limited capacity: you could find the extinguisher starting to run out just as you are getting the fire under control. Dry powder extinguishers, although compact, are not always successful at sea because the powder tends to settle down under the vibration and movement and so they don't always operate when required. Gas or liquid extinguishers of various types are designed for specific kinds of fires, and these are usually the ones specified for motor sailer use, but various countries have regulations concerning both the type and size of extinguisher and the extinguishing substances and it is important to follow the recommended types in the country concerned.

With only limited fire extinguisher capacity on board, you may soon run out of equipment to tackle the fire if you have to confront it. In order to increase firefighting capability, it is worth thinking about having the bilge pump made convertible to a fire pump by adding a sea connection into the system, so that a fire can be tackled using the unlimited quantities of water which surround the boat; though do remember that pumping water into the boat can't go on forever without risking capsizing. Go round the boat and think about how you would tackle particular types of fire. In that way you will get a much better idea about what practical equipment you need and where to locate it.

Distress signals

If things do get out of hand and you have to consider abandoning ship, then you will need to attract attention. Flares are the traditional way of doing this. These come in three types: hand flares, parachute flares and smoke flares. Many countries have regulations or requirements as to what should be carried, but for a motor sailer capable of offshore cruising a minimum of six parachute flares should be carried. These can be supplemented by hand and smoke flares, but the parachute flare is the only one which can be seen for any reasonable distance, and is effective both day and night. Keep the flares stowed where they are ready for quick use, which on a motor sailer usually means in the wheelhouse. Stowage should be dry, and should also be secure so that the flares do not roll around in their stowage. Always respect the expiry date which is stamped on the flares, which generally means renewal every two or three years. Whilst it may seem a shame to throw away what appears to be a perfectly good flare, it is vital that they should work in an emergency.

There is a certain feeling of hit or miss when using flares to indicate that you are in trouble. You may get some acknowledgement from the shore or from another boat, but generally you will have no idea whether they have been seen or not. These days they can be considered a secondary system. The primary way of attracting attention should be by using the radio, since not only can you thereby receive acknowledgement of your distress calls, but you can also explain where you are and what your predicament is. Radios will be discussed later under electronics (See page 148).

Liferafts and lifejackets

Included in the category of equipment for abandoning ship are liferafts, lifejackets and lifebuoys. The average motor sailer is basically a sound and seaworthy boat, but the unexpected can and does happen. With the extended cruising capabilities of a motor sailer, disaster could strike quite a long way from land, and a well-equipped liferaft could mean the difference between life and death. These are fairly expensive pieces of equipment and, if the regulations don't demand that one is carried, then the owner himself has to make the painful decision of whether to or not. If the boat is only used on coastal work, then it would not be unreasonable just to have an inflatable dinghy on board which could double up as a liferaft in an emergency, but in offshore waters the liferaft is essential. If you do your boating in cold conditions, a liferaft should again be considered essential, because of the great risk from exposure. The shelter and warmth and relative safety provided by the liferaft canopy are very necessary in these conditions; a dinghy on its own cannot provide adequate protection, although some dinghies can be obtained with a temporary cover.

Just as important as the liferaft itself is where it is stowed. It should be readily available for launching, which usually means the deck or a cockpit locker stowage. Ideally the liferaft should be capable of simply being slipped overboard when released from its stowage, because while it might look easy in harbour to handle a liferaft and throw it overboard, picture trying to do so on the tossing deck of a motor sailer in wild seas. Launching the liferaft can become a major operation if you have to lift it and throw it over the rails. Stowage on the foredeck is not a particularly good idea: in such an exposed location, the liferaft would need strong lashings, which in turn could hinder easy launching. Positioned here it could also hinder visibility from the wheelhouse. The glass fibre containers used for many types of liferaft offer good protection against the elements and against chafe due to movement, but these containers are not easy to hold or to lash down securely. The trend is now to go towards the cheaper type of liferaft stowage using a valise cover. The transom is a popular place for stowing liferafts on sail boats, but few motor sailers have the type of sloping transom necessary for this stowage to work.

Do remember to make the end of the liferaft painter fast. Ensure too that the lashings are fitted with quick release hooks so that all these things are ready in the event of an emergency. To reduce the risk of theft, liferafts are sometimes padlocked in place in their stowage, but do remember to take off the lock before you go to sea, otherwise the hunt for the key could prove embarrassing, even fatal.

Lifejackets could be considered to be the ultimate line of defence in any emergency situation. There is no doubt that, even if you are unconscious, a good lifejacket will keep you afloat and increase your chances of survival. However, in cold water the limiting factor on survival is much more likely to be exposure rather than keeping afloat, so that lifejackets can only ever be a short-term solution. Whether you wear a lifejacket or not is very much an individual decision, and on a motor sailer there is less likelihood of falling overboard than on an open sailing boat, but in bad conditions the owner or skipper should insist on lifejackets being worn. They should be of a type which does not hamper movement.

There are two main types of lifejacket: the fully inflatable, and that containing some inherent buoyancy. Whilst the latter offers a better degree of protection, the fully inflatable type is a more practical solution, and probably the best compromise because it does not hamper movement. If you do your sailing in cold temperatures, you might also want to consider having survival suits on board to reduce the risk of exposure in an emergency situation. In trying to decide between various items of emergency equipment, it is best to try and assess the sort of survival times which might be necessary before help comes, depending on where you sail, the weather and so on. You could survive for a week in a properly equipped liferaft, but in the water wearing only a lifejacket your survival time might be measured in hours.

Safety harnesses

Prevention is again better than cure in a man overboard situation, and one item of equipment to consider for motor sailers is the safety harness. There should certainly be a couple of these harnesses on board, but in the wheelhouse type of motor sailer they are only needed if you have to go out on deck. In modern designs where the sails can generally be handled from aft, there is less need for harnesses, but in bad conditions they are a sensible precaution. You will tend to wear them only when the boat is under sail because under power there is no need to go outside. At full speed under power a harness could prove dangerous if you fell overboard, because of the injury which could be caused by the sudden jerk on the line. It can be argued that you are safer to float clear and be picked up than be dragged alongside the boat. If you are single-handed and go overboard without a harness, then you must ensure you stay with the boat and still have a means of getting back on board. Strong wires rigged along the deck or the coach roof is the standard system by which safety harnesses are attached.

Lifebuoys and marker buoys

In any man overboard situation, carrying a lifebuoy does offer a means of support for the person in the water. A better approach, though, is to have the quick release marker buoys which are now a feature of safety equipment for sail boats. These often come equipped with lights for night-time use, and provide a good means of marking the position of a survivor in the water whilst you turn round ready to pick him up. Recovery of a person in the water can take longer in a sail boat, so a more effective marker than a lifebuoy is required, but it will depend to a certain extent on whether lifejackets are being worn. Recovering a survivor from the water can be a very difficult operation, and a ladder or a bathing platform may not be a very suitable position from which to attempt it in rough seas, particularly if the person in the water is not able to help themselves. The high topsides of many modern designs also hamper recovery. A strop connected to a halyard can provide a means of winching someone on board, or the main sheet tackle could be used.

With all safety equipment a balance has to be struck. The only way to be really safe is not to go to sea at all, but on the basis that you do, then it is important to take reasonable precautions against any disaster occurring. There is an increasing use of regulation to insist that you carry certain items of equipment on board for emergencies, but in itself carrying equipment does not solve problems. It is, in any case, impossible to carry equipment to meet every contingency; it is knowing how and when to use the equipment that really enables you to cope in any emergency. Think through possible eventualities; analyse and find solutions to the problems these throw up; and practise your reactions to any potential emergency situation. If and when the time comes when you have to cope, then you will have a good idea of what to do and how to do it.

Electronics

Modern electronic equipment can go a long way to helping you reduce the risk of getting into emergency situations by allowing more accurate

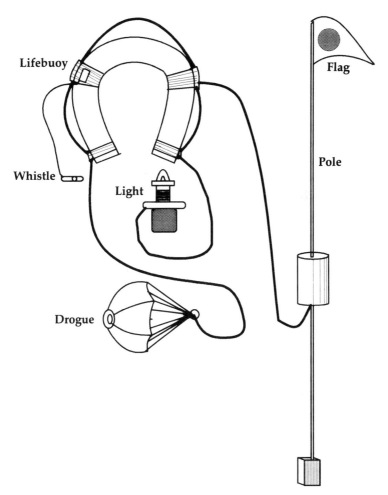

Lifebuoy

Whistle

Light

Drogue

Flag

Pole

FIG 34　A Dan or marker buoy. The pole and flag indicate the position in daylight and the automatic light is for night use. The whistle can help in fog, whilst the lifebuoy provides flotation. The drogue line stabilises the Dan buoy.

and safe navigation and by providing up-to-date weather forecasts and a means for calling assistance should an emergency arise. VHF radio on the marine band is now virtually a standard fitting on all motor sailers and provides a means of keeping in touch with the coastguard, marinas, radio stations, and with other vessels. This should be considered the bare minimum of radio communication equipment, and is suitable for coastal work, but for operations further offshore then an MF or HF SSB radio should be considered. All these radios provide for emergency communications as well as routine calls. You can also use them for making telephone calls via coast radio stations, although more and more motor sailer owners are using cellular phones to gain direct access to the inland telephone systems. A new option for the blue water motor sailer cruiser will be the standard M satellite communication system, which uses a relatively small antenna – just over half a metre in diameter. This can be accommodated on motor sailers over about 40 feet in length and provides good, automatic telephone communications from anywhere in the world into the land line telephone systems. However, calls are expensive, and the cellphone offers probably the best solution for telephone links when you are close to land. Another satellite system operates on the Standard C satellite system, and offers a simple means of making telex links, but this type of communication is not generally required on motor sailers.

Most marine band radios will allow you to pick up emergency calls and navigation warnings as well as weather forecasts, but a dedicated system called Navtex also allows these calls to be picked up automatically and recorded in printed form. This is a positive way of receiving these messages, but the equipment is relatively expensive and does require the installation of a separate antenna which may not always be feasible. The other communications link which is worth considering is a weather fax, which allows weather charts to be received on board. Once again a separate antenna is required.

The location of various antennae requires careful consideration. It is normal to place the VHF radio antennae at the top of the mast because the range of this equipment is little more than line of sight, so the high antenna gives the best range. The same is true of a cellphone antenna; you will certainly get a much better performance away from the land with a masthead antenna. You have a bit more flexibility with the location of these antennae on a ketch-rigged motor sailer because there are two mastheads. Otherwise it can quickly become crowded at the top of the mast, since this is also the optimum place to locate a satellite or terrestrial position fixing system antenna. Wind sensors also have to be accommodated.

With MF or HF radio a larger antenna is required. This can be a whip antenna, perhaps 9 feet or more in length, mounted towards the transom. In some cases the backstay could be used for the antenna if suitable insulators are fitted. Navtex and weather fax receivers require shorter antennae, and these should not be located close to any powerful transmitter antennae such as those from the MF or HF radios. Space can become very much at a premium when trying to locate all the various antennae in their optimum positions, and this can often be the limiting factor in deciding which equipment to carry on board.

One solution to the problem is to have a separate frame like an arch mast or a pole towards the transom, which can be used to mount some of these antennae. A similar arch mast is now a feature on some motor sailers at the rear of the cockpit, where it is used as an attachment point for an overall cockpit cover. These arch masts or poles can provide the antennae with a reasonably clear field of view. They also help to keep the antennae clear of the sailing rig, and provide more space to separate out conflicting antennae. As a general rule it is the radiating transmitting

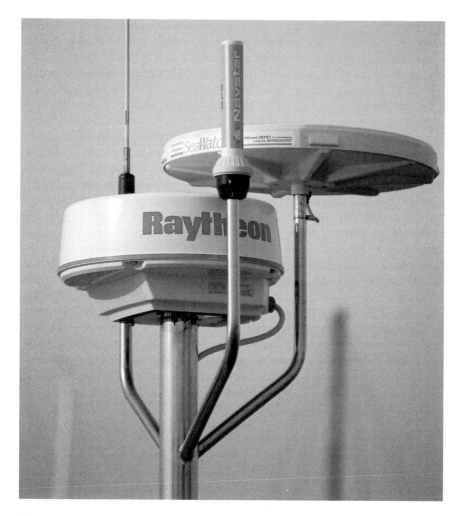

This stern pole carries the antennae for radar, TV reception, GPS and VHF radio. The varying heights of the antennae should reduce interference, although TV reception will probably only be possible when the radar and VHF are not transmitting.

antennae which cause the trouble, and they should be distanced from the receiving antennae.

An antenna problem of a different sort occurs if radar is fitted on board. The antenna here is comparatively large and can be either an enclosed radome or an open rotating antenna. The enclosed dome with its protective cover is probably the best solution, but these tend to be smaller radar antennae which reduce the capabilities of the radar set. For an effective radar, an antenna of at least 3 feet in length should be considered, but finding space to locate it is not always easy. In a ketch-rigged motor sailer, mounting it on the fore side of the mizzen mast is a good solution, whilst the wheelhouse top is another possibility if there is clearance from the boom. On some motor sailers the radar antenna of the enclosed type can be mounted on the fore side of the main mast. Certainly if it is in any location where it is likely to be fouled by ropes, then the enclosed antenna is the only solution. An arch or pole mast at the stern is another good location; to get effective range the radar antenna should be as high as possible.

Another problem concerning the installation of a radar is where to locate the display on board. Certainly it needs to be under cover in the wheelhouse, because radar displays are not usually waterproof. Few motor sailer designs make provision for installing a radar, and therefore it usually ends up on the area between the wheel and the windscreen. This does make it easy to view it from the wheelhouse, but tends to block the view of the outside world. Another solution is to panel-mount the radar if there is space to do so. Radar is certainly a valuable tool, particularly in poor visibility, taking a lot of the guesswork out of navigation. It is the only equipment which can show you surrounding shipping as well as land and navigation mark targets, but it does require a degree of skill to interpret the display, and it doesn't pay to take everything you see on the display at face value. The radar also provides a valuable means of checking your position against that shown by electronic position fixing equipment. Having a radar on board does not do away with the need for a radar reflector, because whilst you can see other

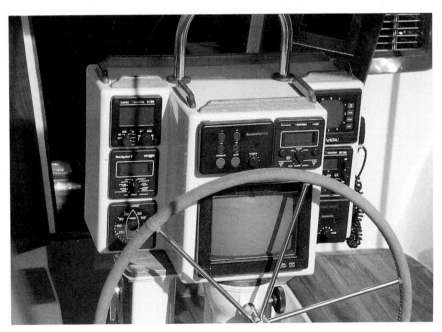

An electronics console at the outside steering position. To be installed in this position, the electronics should preferably be fully waterproof or at least protected from rain and spray. The radar shown here can be particularly useful when navigating in fog or when entering strange harbours.

shipping on your radar, it doesn't necessarily mean that they can see you with the comparatively small radar target that your own vessel presents. So a radar reflector on the mast should be considered an important item of equipment for smaller motor sailers.

Depth, log and wind instruments are the main items of electronics which are now being fitted as standard. This doesn't mean that there isn't a wide choice of different equipment, but tends to be based on the fact that all owners will want this equipment. The echo sounder and log have to have fittings in the hull, and the wind instrument sensors have to be installed at the masthead, so it makes sense for this to be done at the building yard rather than as a retrofit.

Electronic position fixing equipment is now becoming almost a standard fitting on motor sailers, but there is a choice available. In general, the GPS satellite equipment has taken over from the terrestrial systems such as Decca and Loran and the earlier satellite system called Transit. GPS provides reliable positions to an accuracy within 100 metres in most parts of the world, and certainly performs adequately for most motor sailer requirements, particularly in view of the fact that its performance is not affected by weather or other atmospheric conditions. GPS does need an antenna which has a clear view around the horizon so that it can 'talk' directly with the satellites. In mounting the receiver on board it should be placed in an easily accessible position. There are a number of handheld receivers on the market which seem to offer a practical and more flexible alternative to the fixed units, but to work successfully on board a motor sailer these hand units do require an installed antenna. Ideally the display itself should be permanently installed too, so that in the long run you are better off buying a larger, fixed unit anyway. One of the few advantages of the handheld units are that, if you have to abandon ship, it can operate and give your positions using its own self-contained batteries. It can also be used as a means of finding your way back to the ship if you go ashore in a tender in fog. In general, though, these portable systems are probably best used as a back-up to the main receiver. To get reliable results in position fixing you should buy the best quality GPS receiver that you can afford, going for a 5 or 6 channel receiver rather than the cheaper 1 or 2 channel receivers.

Within the limits of current technology the paper chart is still vital for navigation, and there should be a space on board for this to be spread out so that it can be used properly. Finding space for a paper chart is not always easy within the confines of a smaller motor sailer, and the temptation is to use the saloon table down below. This is fine for navigation planning, but for real time navigation you really want the chart in the wheelhouse alongside the steering wheel, particularly when in pilotage waters. The electronic chart is developing rapidly and, provided that the basic plotting is done on the paper chart, then the electronic chart can provide an adequate display for routine navigation. In many ways it is better than the paper chart because it provides a real time plot of the position, showing the direct relationship between where you want to be and where you are, information which is very valuable to the navigator. It becomes even more valuable when used in conjunction with the radar, and there are systems now which allow both radar and electronic chart displays to be combined, although a lot of development is still required to bring these to full effectiveness. The twin screen display of radar and electronic chart gives the navigator nearly all the information he needs at a glance, and the trend in the future is going to be towards three screen displays: one will show the radar, one the electronic chart, and the third will display speed, compass and engine information.

This high reliance on electronics for navigation and monitoring will become a feature of motor sailers, because the equipment can be mounted inside the wheelhouse and kept dry. To obtain the right level of reliability, the power supplies and installation should be carried out to a very high standard. To accommodate the displays there should be adequate space around the steering position or navigating area, something which is often lacking within the confines of the wheelhouse in motor sailers. The trend towards flat screen displays as opposed to the CRT type displays should ease the pressure on space to a certain extent, however, and should also help to improve the reliability of the electronic equipment.

Compasses and autopilots

Even with modern electronics the compass is still a vital piece of equipment. Whilst modern electronics can let you know where you are, the compass is still the main heading reference, and its installation should be given a high priority. A good, well corrected compass is of prime importance, particularly on long passages where a small error in the compass can lead to being a long way out in making a landfall.

Matching the compass to the boat means ensuring that the damping characteristics of the compass card and the way it is pivoted matches the performance of the boat. In general a motor sailer will want a compass which is reasonably well damped, because the motion at times could be lively, particularly going into a head sea. The compass should obviously be placed in front of the helm position; when there are two helm positions, then two compasses are required. There is often a conflict between the requirements for positioning the compass and the fact that it has to be kept at a reasonably safe distance – usually at least half a metre – from electronic equipment. This requirement can often be difficult to achieve within the confines of a motor sailer wheelhouse, where the windscreen wipers and radios can also create magnetic interference. Remember also that magnetic fields can pass through wood and GRP, so if you have a microwave oven in the galley just below the steering position, then this could affect the performance of a compass as well. Other iron and steel objects such as tools, beer cans, etc, can also affect it and, whilst the compass adjuster can do a good job in trying to balance out and eradicate the deviation, it cannot take into account the temporary variations in magnetic fields caused by such objects, or by electronic equipment which may be switched on and off. Getting the compass right is important, so if space is limited and it is not always possible to maintain the recommended safe compass distances, then using an electronic compass should be considered.

The electronic compass still works on the earth's magnetic field, but senses this with coils rather than with the swinging compass needle. It is also affected by outside magnetic influences, but because the output is electronic, the actual sensor unit can be placed in any reasonable position within the boat, so you have a lot more flexibility in where it is mounted. The display itself is not affected by magnetic influences, so it can be located in the optimum position by the steering wheel. Some electronic compasses also incorporate a means of correction: the boat is simply turned through 360 degrees at a steady rate of turn and the compass detects the errors and applies corrections. The original installation should still be looked at by a compass adjuster so that any fixed errors can be eliminated as far as possible, but this automatic correction system does allow you to keep a check on what is going on. The electronic compass is used as a sensor unit for most autopilots today, and this combination of electronic compass and electronic autopilot works well together. A problem to bear in mind with electronic compasses is that they do require a power supply, so any power failure will put the compass out of action, something which doesn't happen with the standard magnetic compass.

Having an autopilot on board can help to add to the pleasure of motor sailing, particularly when you are sailing short-handed. The autopilot takes over the steering and maintains a fixed course, allowing the person on watch to move around the boat and trim the sails or carry out other duties rather than be pinned to the wheel. For many motor sailer owners, the autopilot is an essential piece of equipment: not only can it be used to maintain a steady course, but with the remote, handheld control units for many autopilots, the boat can also be steered using the autopilot controls when negotiating narrow channels or harbours.

We tend to think of autopilots as working only when the boat is under power, but they can also work under sail using either a compass heading as the reference point or steering a course in relation to the wind. The latter can be valuable when sailing close-hauled or when running directly before the wind, but when operating the autopilot under sail, do remember that it puts a drain on the batteries at a time when they are not being recharged.

Alternative power supplies

When the motor sailer is operating under sail alone, electrical power can be provided by using either solar panels, wind generators, or water generators. Solar panels provide a small current, usually enough to keep electronic systems running, by converting the power of the sun's rays directly into electrical current. The solar panels are mounted on flat areas of the deck and are completely automatic in operation. They will also, of course, keep the batteries topped up when the boat is in harbour. The current they produce is minimal, but usually enough to keep things ticking over. Wind generators use a propeller to drive an alternator to supply electrical current. Whilst they don't enhance the aesthetics of a motor sailer, they do provide a viable alternative charging system, with enough output to keep navigation lights and autopilots running even in light wind conditions. Much the same goes for water generators, where a propeller – either fixed to the hull or towed behind the boat – is used to drive a small alternator which provides electrical power. However, unlike the wind generator, which operates when the boat is static, the water generator does need the boat running through the water in order to produce the electrical current.

Navigation lights

Any vessel operating at night must have navigation lights to indicate its whereabouts and its heading. The international regulations for the prevention of collision at sea specifies the minimum range from which these lights must be visible, but for a small boat, the brighter the lights the better. When operating under sail, these lights can provide quite a drain on the battery during night operations, and whilst solar panels won't help supply this current at night-time, wind or water generators will. The lights themselves are often mounted in exposed positions, and must be totally waterproof if they are going to be reliable. On a motor sailer it is not always easy to position these lights where they can be seen when the sails are up; usually the red and green side lights are located on either side of the pulpit forward, or on the wheelhouse top. It is in the latter position that they tend to be obscured by the foresail, and the exposed pulpit mounting is usually the first choice for their position. The white steaming light which is used when the boat is under power can be mounted on the mast, since the sails are not usually up when motoring. When motor sailing, this light should still be carried, and is usually placed at the masthead. The stern light poses fewer problems, and can be mounted either on the aft side of the wheelhouse or on the stern rail, but remember it could be obscured by a dinghy. An alternative to the individual lights on smaller motor sailers is to have a combined light on the masthead. This makes it easily seen, but adds to the competition for space in this restricted area.

Another statutory requirement is to have a fog horn for use underway. This is normally an electrically operated unit, but air-driven types are available. In theory there should also be a bell to ring when the boat is at anchor in fog. A boat proceeding in daylight under motor with the sails up, as could be the case with a motor sailer, is required to show a black conical shape, point down, with a minimum size of 2 feet. This is required by the regulations to indicate that motor sailers follow the rules for powerboats rather than sailing yachts, but few owners take the trouble to show such a shape.

Tenders

The motor sailer makes a fine cruising yacht, which will mean that it will often anchor off small ports and harbours rather than berth alongside. This in turn means having a dinghy on board to get ashore. Rigid dinghies are now rarely carried on board, but rigid inflatables are used on larger motor sailers. Both of these types of tender can create stowage problems on smaller motor sailers. This is why the inflatable is now used almost universally because it can be stowed away safely on long passages or towed on short ones, and it does offer flotation in an emergency. If the inflatable dinghy is being used to double up as a liferaft, it could make sense to have an emergency gas inflation system fitted, because there may not be time to inflate it manually in an emergency situation.

The stowage of the dinghy is never easy. Stowage on deck usually means obstructing visibility from the wheelhouse and it is not always easy to secure a dinghy adequately, particularly in rough conditions when it can present a large surface to any water coming on board. An alternative stowage is in davits over the transom, and this can be practical on moderate sized motor sailers using small dinghies. On double-ended motor sailers, the size and shape of the stern would rule out the use of davits, and the overhang of these davits can also add to your mooring costs in the marina. Towing astern is fine on short passages in reasonable weather, but a dinghy being towed astern can become a liability when the wind is freshening and the sea getting up.

With an inflatable dinghy, it shouldn't be too difficult to find a stowage for it either on deck or in a locker when it is deflated. It may be easier to stow it on deck in a partially deflated state, thus reducing the labour when the dinghy is required for use. If you have an outboard motor on the dinghy, then this is best stowed clamped to a suitable piece of wood, either in the engine compartment if there is space, or better still on the transom rail where the petrol fumes won't cause trouble. If you have an outboard you will also need to find stowage for the fuel tank and other items. This should be in a compartment which doesn't connect to the accommodation or the bilges because of the risk of fumes finding their way below.

Anchors

The provision of anchors, ropes, fenders and other deck gear is largely a matter of common sense. If the motor sailer is used as a serious cruising boat, then an adequate anchor with a spare to back it up should be the

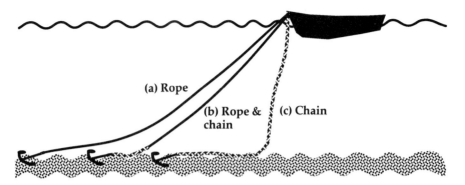

FIG 35 The effect of different anchor line materials: (a) All rope – a more direct pull on the anchor so it needs a longer scope. (b) Combination rope and chain – a compromise between (a) and (c). (c) All chain – the weight gives plenty of spring and a good horizontal pull on the anchor.

minimum requirement. The main anchor should probably be one size larger than the normal recommended size for the size of yacht, bearing in mind that motor sailers can be heavy craft with a fair bit of windage and you may not always be able to choose just when you want to anchor. Since the anchor needed might therefore be heavy, and the crew on a motor sailer when cruising is often small, an anchor windlass should be considered an essential fitting. Such a windlass can be hand, electric or hydraulically operated. The modern ones are compact in design, often with just the heaving head showing above the deck and the motor fitted below decks in the dry. Such a windlass can also double up as a mooring post to relieve the clutter on the foredeck. A real luxury is to have an electric windlass with the control in the wheelhouse, so that you can handle everything by remote control. For this you will need one of the self-stowing types of anchor and a suitable bow fitting which allows the anchor to come into the stowage cleanly. To be successful it should be possible to see what is happening on the foredeck from the wheelhouse.

The list of equipment that you can fit to a motor sailer is almost endless, but before you rush out and buy, think carefully about the benefits that this equipment will bring and, perhaps more importantly, where it is going to be fitted or stowed. It can also be sensible to think about the maintenance aspect of any equipment fitted on board, and also whether there are service agents available locally. When buying a new boat, the equipment and the options on offer should be carefully studied, particularly if the boat has been built abroad. It may not be easy to get some of the equipment serviced or to obtain spares in the country where the motor sailer is operated, although most boat builders do tend to be very careful in this respect and tend to concentrate on fitting equipment which is sold and serviced internationally. It might cost a bit more to go to a reputable company with a long trading history, but 10 years on you may still want to get spares and service for some of the equipment on board, and it may be a lot easier to do this if you deal with an established company.

CHAPTER 11

―――――

COPING WITH EMERGENCIES

Motor sailers are generally sound, safe boats, but at sea you have to be prepared for the worst. In this chapter we will look at some of the emergencies you may have to face when cruising. Obviously we cannot look at every possibility, and the action you take in a particular situation will depend a great deal on the specific situation and the boat involved. Here we will give a broad outline of possible action, but you must view this advice in the context of your own boat and work out how you would handle things. This will make you much better prepared if things do go wrong, especially considering that it is the action you take in the first few moments of an emergency which could well determine the final outcome. This mental preparation will make your instinctive reactions much more positive.

Towing and being towed

When you have to be towed your boat will probably be immobile, so all the manoeuvring will have to be done by the other boat. You can help by getting things ready and making sure that the tow line is secured fast at the first attempt. There is a heavy strain on a tow line, so you need somewhere strong to make it fast. Ideally this should be a good, strong central mooring post at the bow, and the anchor capstan could provide this. However, the stresses on the tow line can be very high indeed and, even if you have a central mooring post, the best solution is to take a couple of turns of the towing line around this post or the capstan and then take the end of the line back to a second securing point, which on a sail boat could be round the mast. In this way the load is spread throughout the hull instead of being concentrated on one point towards the bow. This gives a better chance of the heavy snatches on the line being absorbed safely.

If you have to rely on the mooring cleats on each side of the bow, the best solution is to rig a rope bridle. The bridle should be long enough to pass clear of the bows so that there will be no problem with chafe on the bow roller or anchor; each end of the bridle is made fast to a mooring cleat. Once the tow line is made fast, you can help reduce the strain on the tow line by steering the boat to prevent it from sheering about. This will also help to reduce any chafing problems on the tow line.

Towing a boat is not something to undertake lightly. It calls for skilful manoeuvring and rope handling. If you have to tow another boat, the first stage when you have everything ready is to pass a tow rope across. This is best done with your stern level with the bow of the other boat. Manoeuvre close enough for the line to be thrown across, using a lighter line for the initial contact if this is going to be easier to throw. If the sea and wind conditions are difficult and you are reluctant to get this close to the boat being towed, as could be the case if it has gone aground, then you could float the line down to the other boat using a fender tied to the end of the tow line to keep it afloat and make it visible.

At all times when you are passing the tow line make sure that the rope does not end up around your propeller. You certainly don't want to compound the difficulty in this way. The person handling the line on the stern of your boat must allow just enough slack to enable the line to be passed across; never allow a bight of rope to lie in the water. When you are making the line fast on your stern, you may have to use a bridle to spread the load between the two stern cleats. It is rare to find a good strong towing point on leisure boats these days, and an alternative solution could be to take a couple of turns around a stern cleat and then back it up with further turns around the mast or a bow cleat.

Take up the weight gently on the tow tope once it is fast, and try to keep an even strain, not an easy task in rough seas. Radio contact between the two boats will bring an added measure of safety to the towing operation. You should be able to find a speed of towing at which both boats are comfortable without too much snatching on the line. In calmer conditions you can keep a reasonably short tow line, but in rougher conditions you need to have a longer tow line between the two craft which will give a bit of spring. You can experiment with the length of tow line to find a length which gives a compatible motion between the two craft. If the boat being towed still has steering, then a position somewhere just on the quarter of the towing boat can often be a comfortable place to hold.

When a tow line is being secured at either end, the person handling the rope should wear a lifejacket and safety harness. The latter is probably more important than the lifejacket because you are very vulnerable on the foredeck at sea and you may need both hands to handle the tow line. Falling overboard can only complicate an already tricky situation, so make sure the rope handlers are well protected.

Mast down

Having the mast collapse can be quite a traumatic experience. It tends to happen very suddenly. Your first action should be to reduce the impact of the damage. This means cutting away any remaining rigging which is attached, and preventing the mast knocking a hole in the hull or

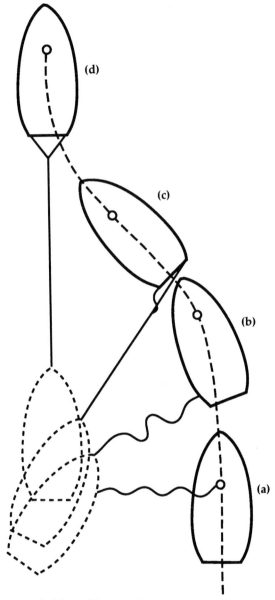

FIG 36 Picking up a tow. At (a) and (b) the tow line is being passed across and connected to the towing bridle at the stern of the towing boat. At (c) the weight is coming on to the tow line, and at (d) both boats are lined up and speed is increased.

damaging fittings. You may want to retain bits of the mast and rigging, and particularly the sails attached to it, in order to erect some sort of jury rig. This will certainly be the case if you are some distance from the land and you don't have enough fuel to get back into harbour using the engine. To solve the immediate problem, you might want to cut away all the rigging, except perhaps the fore or backstay; this will allow the wreckage of the mast and sail to drift away from the boat, but still remain attached. In this way you buy yourself a bit of time in order to sort out what you want back on board, and what your next step is to be. One thing to bear in mind immediately if the mast does go over the side, is that the damping effect of the mast and sails will be lost and you could find the motion of the boat much more lively, which makes any deck activity more difficult. You can start the engine and point the boat up into the wind, but make sure that none of the debris from the rigging, mast or sail gets into the propeller.

Once you have cleared the mast away, you can think about heading for port. If power is not an option because fuel is low, then a jury rig could get you to harbour. You are only likely to make progress, however, with the wind astern, or at least somewhere abaft the beam, and you will need to bear this in mind when planning your course of action and deciding where you are going to head for.

How you set up the jury rig depends on what is left after the dismasting. If you are lucky and the mast broke half-way up, then it is not too difficult to rig some sort of sail to the remains of the mast. Make sure the mast is supported adequately before you impose further strain on it. It might be possible to rig the existing main and a small jib, but an alternative is a form of square sail hung from the boom or spinnaker pole lashed across the mast.

If there is no mast left standing, then it is not easy to rig a single pole from scratch, but you could use a spinnaker pole and part of the mast to rig sheer legs. Wedge the heel of each leg against the toe rail on either side, and use the fore and aft rigging to hold it firmly in place. Just how you set a jury rig will depend on what materials you have available and what the conditions are. Jury rigs sound feasible on paper, but the reality is much more difficult and can require hours of patient work: there are no short cuts to a sound jury rig. The chances are that, if the mast has gone overboard, the winds are strong, and in these conditions rigging a replacement can be extremely difficult, if not impossible. If you have sufficient sea room, then it is probably safer to wait until the sea conditions moderate before attempting this operation.

Man overboard

At first glance, having one of your crew fall overboard seems a straight-forward matter to deal with. You simply turn round and head back and pick him up and away you go. Behind this apparently straightforward solution to the problem lies a whole host of difficulties: you have to locate the person in the water; you have to control your boat and bring it back to the man in the water; and then, probably the most difficult part, you have to get the person back on board. It is all too easy for this situation to turn into a nightmare where lives are at risk.

The first action to take when someone goes overboard is to release or throw a marker. If you have a Danbuoy at the stern then let this go, or a lifebuoy as a second-best choice. Even something like a cockpit cushion could help, because a person in the water is very hard to keep sight of. They can be a very small target in a very big ocean, and by the time you have turned to come back again, finding that person amongst the waves can be a difficult and frustrating task. At night-time the problem is compounded because, without some form of light to indicate their position, finding the person in the water is obviously even more difficult. The Danbuoy with its light and flag on a pole is a vital piece of equipment in this situation. The casualty is marked and is provided with buoyancy for support. Now you can think about recovery.

If a person goes overboard forward, turning the wheel towards the side on which they went over can help to keep the casualty clear of the propeller, but you will have to be quick if this is to have any worthwhile effect. The next step is to post one of the crew on deck, whose sole task is to keep sight of the person in the water. This requires keen concentration; he should not be distracted from this task for any reason, since once sight is lost, finding the person again will be that much more difficult. Remember that the time gap between the person going overboard and launching the Danbuoy can mean that they could be separated by quite a distance.

Now comes the problem of turning and heading back. On a motor sailer the only sensible solution is to stop by going astern on the engine, turn the boat short round, and head back. This quick turn will mean that you will probably not travel more than 100 metres from the casualty. An alternative is a manoeuvre called the Williamson Turn. This involves putting the helm hard over towards the side the casualty went over until the course is altered through 60 degrees from the original heading. Then you apply full opposite rudder until the boat comes round on a reciprocal course to the original course. This manoeuvre should bring you straight back to the person in the water. It was developed for use by larger vessels

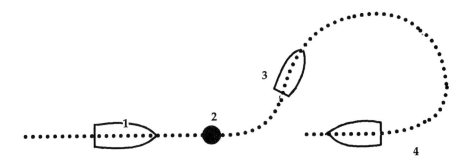

FIG 37   The Williamson Turn for recovering a man overboard casualty. (1) is the original course. (2) is the point where the man overboard occurs. At this point the helm is put hard over towards the side where the person has fallen to try to keep him clear of the propeller. (3) when the heading has swung through 60°, in this case from 090° to 030°, the helm is then put hard over in the opposite direction. (4) the boat comes round on to the original track and the man overboard should be right ahead.

which cannot stop quickly, but small boats with their rapid stopping capability and quick turning should simply stop and turn round. This is good for the morale of the person in the water, and will also make it much easier to keep him in sight. There is nothing more reassuring to the man overboard than seeing the boat stop and turn quickly. He will then know not only that he has been spotted, but that recovery is imminent. Seeing a boat going away in a wide sweeping turn can be quite alarming, and could lead to the person in the water panicking, reducing his chances of survival.

If you have the sails up then you can leave them up and make the recovery under engine whilst head-to-wind. However, although dropping the sails means heading up into the wind before making the recovery, and will take a few moments longer, it will give you better control during the recovery process, and is therefore a better option. It also reduces the chance of a line around the propeller.

Recovering the casualty when you are head-to-wind reduces the risk of the boat drifting over the casualty in the water. This could happen if you try to pick him up on the lee side, whilst with a recovery on the weather side you may not be able to get close enough alongside.

These manoeuvres are fine if you can keep the casualty in sight, or at least the Dan marker buoy that you have put overboard. If you have an electronic position finding receiver on board, then make an immediate note of the position of the man overboard situation. Some of these receivers have a man overboard button which automatically records the position and gives you the course and distance back to that position. This can be a great help, particularly at night-time and if there is no light on the casualty.

Having got back alongside the person in the water, you are still faced with the problem of recovery. Even when the casualty is conscious and can help himself, trying to lift a waterlogged person back on board is an almost impossible task. The first thing is to secure the casualty alongside to make sure he stays there and has some support while you organise recovery. A bight of rope under the armpits and round the back and made fast on board will do this. You may then be able to get a second rope around the casualty's legs to pull him horizontal and into a position where you can think about rolling him on board. It won't be easy, particularly if you are the only person left on board, or if there is a weak crew. Alternatively you can rig a tackle from the boom and lift the person on this tackle. The third method is to use a sail as a sling by getting it underneath the casualty and lifting him in it. It all sounds easy enough, but in reality it is incredibly difficult to get someone on board.

Your boat might have a bathing platform at the stern which could facilitate recovery. If you use this area for recovery, always bring the casualty alongside at the side and then transfer him to the stern once the engines are stopped. It is often possible to get close to the waterline at the stern, but if this doesn't work then think about using the dinghy for recovery. Launch the dinghy and recover the casualty first into that, and then transfer the casualty from the dinghy to the boat. Bear in mind that if the casualty is helpless, then recovery becomes that much more difficult. If the casualty is unconscious, then your priority should be mouth-to-mouth resuscitation before recovery. This will entail somebody going into the water to help, or at least reaching the casualty with a dinghy.

There are so many permutations and possibilities with recovery that there is no easy and simple solution applicable to all situations. Man overboard is certainly a situation that you should practise with your crew in good conditions, and only then will you start to appreciate the problems involved, and also be able to work out possible solutions applicable to your particular craft.

Grounding

If a boat goes aground, then the action you take will depend a great deal on the type of bottom on which it goes aground and the prevailing sea conditions. Going aground in the confines of a harbour or estuary are more likely to hurt your pride than the boat itself. Here it is a question of running the engines astern to try and get the boat off immediately, or waiting until the tide floods sufficiently to lift the boat off the bottom. Going aground out in the open sea when there is wave motion is a more serious situation, and going aground on rocks can be even more serious because of the risk of hull damage. There is also the risk of damage to the stern gear, which can compound your problems. Grounding can produce a wide variety of situations that you may have to cope with, some immediate and serious, others requiring patience and seamanship.

The first action on the boat grounding is to try and get it off again immediately. Under sail a motor sailer will probably be heeling over as it goes aground due to the pressure of the wind in the sails. When heeled, the draft is reduced, so by the time you get the sails down you will be well and truly aground. Putting the engine in reverse and trying to power the boat off is unlikely to be effective. If you have gone aground when under engine alone, then reversing the engine is the first step to take to try and get the boat back into deeper water. By hanging a weight such as the tender or a crewman on the end of the boom it might be possible to heel the boat enough for it to come off the bottom, otherwise it is a case of waiting for the tide to float the boat.

The propeller on a motor sailer is generally well protected against damage, and you have plenty of power available to try and drag the boat off. If this immediate action to get the boat off is not successful, then you need to plan a longer term strategy. The first thing you need to know is what the tide is doing. If it is flooding, then maintaining the engines running astern will let the tide lift the boat and get you out of trouble. On a falling tide, you may be able to run out an anchor quickly in the direction of deeper water: hauling on this anchor line, together with the use of the engines, may be enough to drag the boat off the shallow

FIG 38   How the draft can be reduced by hanging a weight on the end of the swung out boom. This is one method of trying to get a grounded vessel afloat, but it is not likely to work if you grounded with the sails up because the boat would already have been heeled over.

bottom before the tide drops too far. Laying out the anchor has to be done with a dinghy, and the best way to do this is to have the anchor hanging over the side of the dinghy with the chain lashed on board by means of a light line which can quickly be cut to let the anchor go. Once you are aground it may be better to wait until the sea bed dries out and then simply walk the anchor away.

On a falling tide, where your immediate actions have not been enough to get the boat off the bottom, then you still need to lay out an anchor, particularly if there is any wind blowing. This will prevent the boat blowing harder aground, and it will also hold the boat secure when the tide starts to flow and the boat floats off the bottom. When you do lay out an anchor, try and put as much scope out on the cable as possible to ensure that the anchor holds well, and keep a steady strain on the cable. When the tide eventually starts to lift the boat, steadily wind in the cable as the boat gradually floats off the bottom. You will soon find yourself in deeper water, ready to start the engine and return to normality.

If you are stuck hard and fast aground and have to wait over the tide, then one of the problems you will have to face is that the boat will heel over as the tide drops unless you have bilge keels. This is the time to rig legs if you carry them on board so that the boat will sit upright over the low water.

Many motor sailers will lie over on their bilge reasonably happily in terms of structural stress when grounded, as long as the sea bed is reasonably smooth. Life on board will not be particularly comfortable at this angle. Because you have not chosen the resting place for the hull, hull damage could occur if the bilge of the boat rests on rocks or other obstructions under water, and as far as possible you should check that the bottom is smooth and obstruction free. You might like to try fixing bunk cushions or fenders at the turn of the bilge before the boat heels over to cushion the impact. Your most important course of action when drying out is to try and get the boat to lie head-to-wind and sea. Then, when the tide starts to flood, waves will not break over the side of the boat and start to fill the hull. Even then you must be prepared for the water to rise quite alarmingly over the edge of the deck before the hull starts to return towards the upright.

When the boat heels over at this angle, check that fuel is not leaking from the fuel tank breathers or fillers. Batteries should also be checked for security and leakage. If you go aground on a soft, muddy bottom, the boat will probably sit more upright as the keel first sinks well into the mud, but here you must check that mud has not blocked the water intake before you start the engine.

Grounding out in the open sea, particularly on rocks, is a serious problem. It is certainly one where a distress call should be sent off as one of your priorities. You may manage to get off without outside help, but the chances are that, even if you achieve this, there will be damage to the boat or to the hull. The knowledge that outside help is on its way can therefore be very reassuring: it is better to have help on its way and then find you don't need it, rather than to wait until the situation is more serious and then calling for help. When you have gone aground in this way it will either be through a propulsion failure or a navigation mistake; in either case the method and position of your grounding will not be of your choice. If you have engines available then try and use these to get the boat off immediately. The other priority, apart from ensuring the immediate safety of yourself and your crew, is to try and get an anchor out to at least hold the boat in position and prevent it drifting further ashore. This anchor will also help to keep the boat head-to, or stern-to-wind and sea. Again the dinghy is the only means of getting the anchor out unless you have outside help, and you must assess the risks of using the dinghy in these conditions before embarking on this undertaking. The safety of your crew must be your number one priority. You should therefore also get safety equipment ready for immediate use.

Fire

There are plenty of highly combustible materials on board a yacht which can fuel a fire. As discussed in Chapter 9, prevention is obviously better than cure, and there we looked at some of the safety precautions and firefighting equipment likely to prove most valuable. Here we shall look at coping with a fire if it does break out.

Provided it is discovered early and you have appropriate extinguishers, the fire itself should not be too much of a hazard. The risks from fire tend to come more from the associated smoke and fumes than from the flames themselves. Bunk cushions and other furnishings can generate large quantities of toxic fumes when on fire, and an electrical short circuit behind panelling could have the same effect if there is foam insulation. These fumes can be so dense that they can force the crew to evacuate the compartment. If this happens, then the crew can't get to the seat of the fire to tackle it and the situation can escalate rapidly. This is the real danger with fire on board yachts, and it highlights the need to get to a fire in its early stages and tackle it quickly.

For a fire to burn it needs oxygen, heat and fuel. Take away one of these and the fire will go out. For instance, water put on a fire will remove heat by generating steam; this steam will displace the oxygen. Water is therefore a good fire extinguishing medium. Most fire extinguishers work on the basis of excluding the oxygen which will stop the fire burning. However, with extinguishers there is always the risk that once the extinguishing gas or liquid has dispersed, oxygen will be able to get back to the seat of the fire and so you can find the fire flaring up again. This is because the other two factors required for fire, heat and fuel, have not been eliminated.

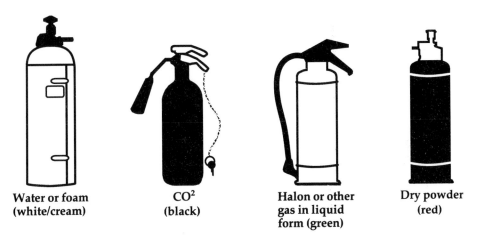

Water or foam   **CO²**   **Halon or other**   **Dry powder**
(white/cream)   **(black)**   **gas in liquid**   **(red)**
                                            form (green)

FIG 39   Some of the alternative types of fire extinguisher. These are the types which conform to DoT requirements; those for motor sailer use would tend to be smaller and capable of one handed use.

We have seen in Chapter 9 that fire extinguishers need to be located outside the compartment they are meant to protect. This allows you to tackle the fire from outside the compartment, keeping your escape route open. If you suspect that the fire is electrical in origin, then turn off the batteries at the main switch to try and isolate the circuits so that the initial cause of the fire is removed. In a galley fire, try and switch off the gas or other combustibles, so once again the basic fuel for the fire is removed. In the engine compartment both fuel and electrical circuits should be isolated. If you get to the fire early enough then an extinguisher should be adequate to put out the fire, but remember that on a yacht you are not dealing with a nice comfortable, stable situation. One of your first reactions on discovering a fire will probably be to stop the engine or head up into the wind. You have to try and visualise fighting a fire in a yacht which may be rolling around quite heavily at sea. Fire extinguishers must have adequate capacity to cope with a severe fire, but must also be light enough to operate one handed because you may need the other hand for holding on.

On a boat you are of course surrounded by one of the best firefighting mediums, water. This will cope with most fires on board, except those involving fuel and probably galley fires. Whilst the fire is being tackled by fire extinguishers, have buckets of water ready in the cockpit to reinforce the fire extinguishers. It may make a mess, but that is far preferable to having the boat burned down to the waterline. If the fire is in a mattress or other bedding, then the most expedient way of dealing with it may simply be to drag the offending item out into the cockpit and dump it overboard.

The fumes generated by a fire are likely to be much more of a problem than the fire itself, and we have already seen that these can prevent access to the fire to extinguish it. If fumes become a major problem, one approach is to seal off the compartment involved, blanking off as many ventilators and openings as possible, and simply allowing the fire to burn itself out as it becomes starved of oxygen. Burning foam, whether from a mattress or from insulation, produces very unpleasant toxic fumes which could quickly overcome a crew member fighting a fire down below. On a powerboat these fumes could quickly reach the wheelhouse to cause further problems. The fumes can be controlled to a certain extent by running downwind, which will tend to keep the stern of the boat clear of the fumes, and will also tend to prevent the flames from reaching this area, at least in the short term. This will keep at least part of the boat still habitable, and give you a better chance to sort out the situation.

In any fire situation, the priorities should be first to tackle the fire itself as quickly as possible, and secondly to send off a distress message. With an electrical fire, you will have to shut down the electrical circuits, which will make it impossible to send a radio distress message. This situation makes a good case for having a portable, hand-held radio readily available on board as a secondary line of communication. Make sure that all abandon ship equipment and items such as distress flares are well away from the seat of the fire and ready for rapid use. Fire has a disconcerting habit of suddenly breaking through bulkheads or the deck, and flaring up with increased rapidity. What to do if the fire gets completely out of control is covered in the section on abandoning ship.

Loss of steering

Loss of the steering is a frustrating and potentially dangerous situation. You could possibly steer the boat by altering the balance in the sails, but the alternative is to try and rig some form of jury rudder. Like a jury sail rig, this is one of the more difficult operations you can be faced with at sea. A lot depends on what equipment you have available to do the job. It could be possible to rig a spinnaker pole as a jury rudder, provided you can attach a blade of some sort to one end and have lines taken to each side of the stern to pull it one side or the other. It is a pretty crude set-up which may not last for too long through chafe and other problems. Using the boom is another possibility, and you will need to look around the boat to see what might be available for the job.

Fortunately, a complete steering failure is comparatively rare these

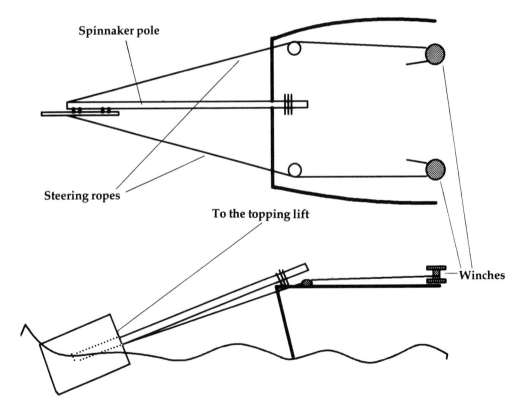

FIG 40 Rigging a jury rudder will never be easy and much will depend on the materials available. Here is one idea with the two ropes led to sheet winches.

days, and it is more likely that part of the steering system itself will fail: the tiller might break, for example, or the steering connection between a wheel and the rudder stock fail. Most rudder stocks where they come through the boat have a square end, and provision is often made for a tiller to be attached to the rudder stock at this point so that effective steering can be maintained. In some cases only a short tiller can be fitted, to which it may be necessary to rig tackles or lines taken to winches to help with the steering. If there is no emergency tiller as such, you may be able to make a connection by using a large spanner clamped on to the tiller, or disconnect the steering system from the existing tiller inside the stern and attach lines or tackles to that. Again it is really a question of looking at the possibilities on your particular boat, working out what is feasible and practical and making sure that you have adequate equipment on board to cope with the situation should it occur at sea.

Abandoning ship

There are three main situations where you may be forced to consider abandoning ship. One is when the vessel is on fire, another is when you have suffered a failure of machinery, mast or steering and the boat is drifting ashore, and the third is when the boat is holed or sinking. These can all be pretty desperate situations, but even so you want to save making the transition from the yacht into the liferaft until the last possible minute. Taking to the liferaft is an irrevocable step which doesn't offer you immediate salvation, and you will always be better off staying on board the yacht whilst it remains tenable and afloat.

Taking to the liferaft when the yacht is on fire poses particular problems. In any evacuation situation it would be normal to put the liferaft over on the lee side, which not only helps to make boarding easier, but also allows the liferaft to drift away downwind once the crew are on board. With the boat on fire, though, the lee side is the last place you want to be, because smoke and flames will blow down to leeward. If you put the liferaft over on the windward side it is less at risk, but getting away from the side will be very difficult. The alternative, and probably the best solution in this situation, is to put the liferaft over either at the bow or the stern, depending where the seat of the fire is located and the heading of the yacht. If the fire is in the forepart of the boat, then obviously you want to evacuate at the stern, and vice versa. Getting into the liferaft over the bow may not be an easy operation, but it could be a better option than trying the same exercise amongst the smoke and flames at the stern. Even then you need to be particularly careful when you slip the painter and let the liferaft drift away.

The key to successful evacuation in a fire situation is to make an early decision to evacuate. Almost certainly a fire will have started down below rather than on deck, and if you resolve to abandon ship before the fire spreads to the hull and superstructure then you should have a good chance of getting out safely. If you wait until the last possible moment when flames are raging in the cockpit, or licking through cabin windows, then your chances of a safe evacuation are considerably reduced. If you have exhausted all the fire extinguishers and any other means of extinguishing the blaze and the fire is still growing, then there is little more you can do. In that situation, the sooner you get into the liferaft the better.

Another situation which can pose problems when you are thinking about abandoning ship is when you are drifting down on to a lee shore. You may have lost your engines and your rig and be unable to control the boat so that it is drifting down to leeward uncontrollably. Your last resort here will be the anchor, which may be adequate to hold you when it can touch bottom. Whilst anchors are normally used for holding the motor sailer off a pleasant beach or in a sandy cove, the anchor has a vital emergency role to play when you are drifting, and it can remain the one last chance between you and disaster. The anchor can reduce the feeling of helplessness when you are drifting uncontrollably; it is here that you will appreciate the virtues of having a larger than usual anchor and a line strong enough to give the anchor a chance to hold in these stressful conditions. If you are already in shallow enough water, the anchor should be used at the earliest possible moment to arrest the drift of the yacht. Under the stress of strong wind and sea conditions, the anchor may not hold securely at the first try. There is a good chance it will grip as the water shoals; the sooner it gets a grip on the bottom, the more time you will have to await rescue.

Buying time in this way is an important consideration, and you should study the chart to see whether there could be better holding conditions further inshore. Good holding ground in deeper water might be better than a rocky bottom in shallow water inshore. On balance, it is good holding ground which provides the key to using the anchor in an emergency. You should also wait until the water is reasonably shallow, say down to 10 metres, so that the anchor has a good chance of holding securely with the anchor line in a relatively shallow catenary. This is the ideal, but when you are drifting ashore your choices may be limited. It could be that, off a steeply shelving coastline, the only option is to put the anchor line over the side with a nearly full scope and wait in the hope that it will catch somewhere before you drift on to the rocks or into the surf region. It is difficult to give hard and fast criteria for using the anchor in this way, because so much will depend on the conditions and water depths, but these are scenarios which are worth rehearsing mentally because you may have only one chance for the anchor to hold and you want to take full advantage of that chance.

Once the anchor has got a hold then you can wait patiently for help to arrive, provided you have got a distress message away or you are reasonably confident that your plight has been observed. Alternatively, you might have to think about trying to organise your own salvation, particularly if the anchor starts to drag. When a yacht is drifting ashore, you are really faced with two alternatives. One is to stay with the yacht and let that take the impact before you try and scramble through the surf or over the rocks on to dry land; the other is to take to the liferaft and try and get ashore in that. It is not an easy decision to make because there are no guarantees about the outcome of either course when you make the decision. However, as a broad guide, if the coastline is rocky then you are probably best to stay with the boat and let that take the impact on the rocks before you try and get ashore, either by using the liferaft or simply by scrambling. If it is a question of getting through a heavy surf line, then the liferaft could provide the better option, although a motor sailer with an anchor down but dragging ashore could provide a reasonably safe habitat through the surf. Liferafts are not particularly comfortable in surf conditions, where the drogue line is rarely strong enough to react against the massively increased pull as the liferaft is attacked by the breakers; there is always the risk of capsize in these conditions. One possible solution is to attach the liferaft to the boat using a long line, abandon ship just outside the surf line, drifting ashore in the liferaft which will still be attached to the abandoned yacht. This could provide you with a more secure method of getting through the heavy surf.

In any sort of emergency at sea you will have to be prepared to take the initiative. The outcome of the situation will depend to a great extent on your decisions, particularly those you make in the early stages. To have a reasonable chance of getting them right, you have to prepare for them. Preparation comes in many forms: it involves having a safe and sound boat, in trying to anticipate what might go wrong and how to cope if it does, and in having the correct equipment on board to tackle problems. There are plenty of people waiting to help you if things do go wrong, but you should aim to be as self-sufficient as possible and that will only come from meticulous preparation.

CHAPTER 12

———

THE FUTURE

The modern motor sailer has developed from its fishing boat origins into a sophisticated cruising craft. As we have seen, the ancestors of the design can still be detected in some of the hull shapes and propulsion systems, but modern materials, sails and engines have changed the motor sailer concept dramatically.

Today the motor sailer designer's job is one of refinement, making use of new and better materials rather than making do with many of the compromises of the past. This process of design refinement may mean the motor sailer becomes less and less a recognisable type of craft. Already we are seeing the divisions between the motor sailer and the cruising yacht starting to disappear as far as performance is concerned, and at the sailing end of the motor sailer market, the motor sailer is becoming recognisable only by the fact that shelter in the form of a wheelhouse is provided for the crew. On sail boats, steering canopies have been replaced by fixed shelters, which starts to bring them into motor sailer territory; the deck saloon sailboats being introduced by many builders blur the divisions even more.

It is in the motor orientated side that the traditional virtues of the motor sailer persist. Modern designs in this sector demonstrate that power and sail can be combined in a practical and viable design, which because of its traditional appearance still has wide appeal. With a general trend in modern design towards reflecting on traditional standards, the motor orientated motor sailer stands out as an excellent example of how traditional concepts can be married to modern materials and design features. The pronounced sheer line and the upright wheelhouse are the hallmarks of the motor orientated motor sailer, but in modern designs they are matched to a soft bow and alloy mast and spars. Tan sails are often used to extend the traditional appearance, but these sails are made from modern materials.

To a certain extent the wheel has turned full circle. As divisions between the motor sailer and sail boats disappear, the more traditional designs remain the last toehold of the displacement motor cruiser concept, since modern motor cruisers have moved towards the light-weight planing boat hull even for displacement use. So in true motor sailer designs the virtues of the heavy displacement hull are still recognised, and this could be a growth area of the leisure market as owners look for stability in design in a fast changing world. The future for development of this traditional concept is limited, but that is part of its attraction.

One area for development would be the introduction of twin screw propulsion. This is already being done on larger motor sailers almost as a matter of course. On a smaller motor sailer, twin screw propulsion would improve manoeuvrability in harbour and give redundancy in the event of a failure at sea, but against this has to be weighed the increased cost and complication and, perhaps more importantly, the smaller propellers which would result in reduced thrust in rough conditions. Perhaps the main argument against it is that it is a break from the tradition which is becoming an essential feature of motor sailer design, although the compact, high powered diesel engines now on the market make twin engined motor sailers a practical proposition in smaller sizes.

Attempts to produce a planing motor sailer have used twin engines. Whilst such concepts can be made to work, and with modern lightweight power units would become even more practical in the future, such a concept is a contradiction. It is difficult to picture an owner who wants a 25 knot powerboat which can sail, and certainly any design of this type would be less seaworthy than the traditional hull concepts. The need to keep weight down would mean serious compromises in the design.

This does not mean, however, that higher performance has to be ruled out from future motor sailer design both under power and sail. Many modern catamarans, with their twin screw propulsion and comfortable accommodation, are effectively motor sailers; these would appear to be the answer for an owner who wants higher performance. With a modern design, it would be possible to get 15 knots under power and sail from a catamaran motor sailer, and under power alone it could be boosted to 25 knots without too much difficulty.

Where the catamaran falls down in many people's eyes is in its appearance. It is not an easy job to make a catamaran look attractive, particularly to the more conservatively minded yachtsmen, but one of the future areas of development is likely to be in this aspect of catamaran design, trying to balance the concepts of speed and tradition.

In the monohull design area, there is a lot of scope for development under water. Whilst motor sailers tend to have a moderate draft, there is scope for developing motor sailers with a shallow draft to help widen their cruising area. Shallow draft is needed not so much when sailing but for entering small harbours. The motor sailer is primarily a cruising yacht, and one of the joys of cruising is to explore small, undeveloped harbours. A shallow draft combined with the ability to sit comfortably on the bottom could be considered an essential criterion by many cruising yachtsmen. Whilst bilge keel hulls meet these requirements to a certain extent, the use of centreboards or drop keels could give even greater versatility and cruising scope.

Above decks, much of the development is likely to revolve around the wheelhouse or wheel shelter. There will be times when you want to be outside sailing in good weather, and times when you want to be inside in the warm and dry protected from the elements. This requirement is generally met by having two alternative steering positions. Having two steering positions adds to the cost and complication and also takes up valuable space on board. An alternative would be to have a wheelhouse or shelter which can be opened up when the weather is fine and closed up when protection is needed. Today this is mainly done by using canvas screens, which do not always make a perfect seal to keep out the wind and the rain. An effective wheelhouse which can be opened up when required is a challenge to the designers.

Electronics are now an essential feature of modern yachting, and the use of electronics is likely to increase in the future. At present electronics are used in an individual way, some for navigation and some for communications. The future path of electronics lies with integration and we will see motor sailers with a three-screen layout comprising radar, electronic chart and information screen. With the increasing use of powered sail handling systems, the way becomes open for the electronic or automatic control of motor sailer sails plus the integration of the engine and sail power. Many may see this as an unwanted development, but it is technically possible. The question is, do we want this level of automation in what is a leisure activity?

In general, motor sailer design, by its very nature, tends to shy away from extremes. The motor sailer of the future may adopt one of the more fashionable names such as 'pilot house sail boat' or 'deck saloon cruiser', but the traditional virtues of comfortable cruising will remain the hallmark of the concept. The extremes which have been produced in the past, such as the planing motor sailer, have not stood the test of time, and the path for future motor sailer development is likely to be one of refinement rather than revolution.

INDEX

OTHER TITLES AVAILABLE FROM ADLARD COLES NAUTICAL

☐ Sails 6th Edition   £27.95
☐ Rigging   £13.99
☐ Boat Electrical Systems   £12.99
☐ Boatowner's Mechanical and Electrical Manual   £30.00
☐ Propeller Handbook   £17.99
☐ Fitting Out 4th Edition   £9.99
☐ Laying Up Your Boat   £7.99
☐ Osmosis and the Care and Repair of Glassfibre Yachts   £11.99
☐ Effective Skippering   £14.99
☐ Heavy Weather Sailing 4th Edition   £30.00
☐ A Guide to Small Boat Radio   £12.99

All these books are available or can be ordered from your local bookshop or can be ordered direct from the publisher. Simply tick the titles you want and fill in the form below.

Prices and availability subject to change without notice

Send to: Adlard Coles Nautical Cash Sales, PO Box 11, Falmouth, Cornwall TR10 9EN

Please send a cheque or postal order for the value of the book and add the following for postage and packing.

UK including BFPO: £1.00 for one book plus 50p for the second book and 30p for each additional book ordered up to a £3.00 maximum.

OVERSEAS INCLUDING EIRE: £2.00 for the first book, plus £1.00 for the second book, and 50p for each additional book ordered.

OR Please debit this amount from my Access/Visa Card (delete as appropriate).

Card number

Amount £ _____

Expiry date _____

Signed _____

Name _____

Address _____

_____

Fax no: 0326 376423